Children Around The World

Jane Caballero, Ph.D.
Derek Whordley, Ph.D.

Humanics Limited * Atlanta

HUMANICS LEARNING
The Most Trusted Name in Education
Humanics Learning is an imprint of Humanics Limited

P.O. Box 7447
Atlanta, Georgia 30309

Library of Congress Card Catalog Number: 82 - 81892

PRINTED IN THE UNITED STATES OF AMERICA

ISBN: 0 - 89334 - 112 - 6

Dedication

*To Lara, whose doll collection
added greatly to the book
and to Alma, whose studies
of children around the world
have been an inspiration.*

Contents

About The Authors

Most of the information in this book was acquired by the authors as they traveled in the various countries discussed. Dr. Caballero has been to more than twenty-five countries. She has participated in such educational travel programs, including extension classes, as the European Art and Architecture, Urban Memorials and Artifact Preservation Program at Western Illinois University; The World Organization for Preschool Education (OMEP) study tour of Israel; a Caribbean cruise and Friends of Jamaica program; and the World Organization of Aerospace Education trip to the Soviet Union. She is also a recent recipient of a Fulbright Scholarship to India.

Dr. Caballero's first year of teaching was in a multiethnic classroom in Honolulu, Hawaii. She has also studied the cultural history of Hawaii at Brigham Young University. She taught extension classes for the University of Miami in Freeport and Nassau, in the Bahamas for four years, and has given workshops for the Miccosukee Indians in South Florida. She has studied Spanish, visited Mexico and taught in the Cuban Bilingual Program at the University of Miami. She was on the Multicultural Committee at Morris Brown College, Atlanta University Center, and developed a course there in Multicultural Human Relations. She is chairperson for the Georgia Association on Young Children and member of the Southern Association on Children Under Six multi-cultural committees.

Dr. Whordley has traveled extensively throughout Western Europe and parts of the Middle East and North America. He was a teacher of young children in the United Kingdom and the headmaster of an international primary school in Ankara, Turkey.

Foreword

Many of the attitudes children form about the peoples of other nations stay with them for life. It is important for parents and teachers to help children build positive attitudes toward those who live in other parts of the world.

The authors of *Children Around The World* have provided rich resources for broadening children's knowledge of people in many different countries: people who are like themselves in many ways, yet with differences that make the kaleidoscope of world cultures interesting.

The games, songs, dances, recipes and other activities in this book will help children to see that children all over the world enjoy many of the same things. They have the same human emotions. Yet there are differences due to geography, religion, government, tradition and other factors which should be appreciated and understood. The most important thing children can learn, however, is that no matter where people live, they have much in common with humanity as a whole and their destinies are linked with those of their fellow human beings. When we help dispel stereotyping and prejudices, as this book does, we help children discover that they have friends all over the world.

Alma W. David, Ed. D.
Professor Emeritus,
University of Miami
Coral Gables, Florida

Acknowledgments

We would like to thank the following students in Dr. Whordley's Early Childhood Social Studies course at Mercer University in Atlanta for contributing ideas and for testing recipes and games during the spring of 1981:

Patricia Stewart—Canada and Netherlands

Carolyn Cotton—China

Linda Hynes—Japan and Nigeria

Flora Bargeron—Thailand

Deborah Little—Australia and Russia

Deborah Jamison—Vietnam

Lois Stellern and Rhonda Finfrock—Mexico

Bonnie Meddern—Kenya, Netherlands, and Poland

Sheila Schwartz—Israel and Greece

Angela Sexstone—Iran and Sweden

June McPherson—Spain

Glenna Bender—Italy

Nola Greenway—Switzerland and Denmark

Patricia Grey—France

Kimberly Baker—West Germany, Greece and England

Mary Anne Aldrich—Scotland and Poland

Johanna Rhoades—Ireland and Israel

Special thanks to Karson Leitch for research on the 1990 revision of CHILDREN AROUND THE WORLD

Introduction

Knowledge and awareness of other cultures should be an integral part of every child's education. A significant part of education is the realization that one's own way of life or culture is only one of many in the world. Moreover, understanding different cultures of people throughout the world can lead to a greater appreciation of one's own heritage. The United States has been and continues to be a "melting pot" for many nationalities. Knowledge and appreciation of other countries and cultures help the child relate to other people within the United States. Prejudice is a reflection of fear and/or a lack of understanding. Therefore, children's exposure to other cultures ultimately may help to eliminate some of the negative attitudes in our society.

The format of information with respect to each country consists of: background information, an activity page which includes a map to be used to locate and identify points of interest, and a flag which can be colored. A study of the geographical location and size of a country and its relationship to other countries leads to a better understanding of the country itself and the people within. Knowledge and appreciation of uniqueness in each country can subsequently lead to respect for uniqueness in individuals.

The format for each country may also include a dance or song. Music is an inherent form of human expression and dances and songs are an integral part of the heritage of many countries. In some cultures, dances or songs are a part of religious celebrations. By attempting to learn a particular dance or song, the children actively participate in the learning process. This active participation enables them to relate more fully to the people within the country that they are studying.

A simple vocabulary list has been included for each country. Such a list exposes children to the existence of languages other than English. The alphabets of many languages are made up of different letters from the ones that make up the English alphabet. We have included a few of these alphabets to highlight the differences among cultures.

For each country we have also included a brief section that describes some popular foods and a few simple recipes which may be prepared in the classroom or at home. NOTE: See the Bibliography (page 169) for the source of any recipe marked with an asterisk (*) or asterisks (**). Ethnic personality is reflected in a country's food. Since children especially enjoy cooking and eating, exposing them to different foods is an effective way to enrich their overall understanding of a particular country.

In the primary curriculum, much of the school day is dedicated to reading and math. Social studies should not be neglected, however. Furthermore, math, reading and language experiences can be integrated into this social studies curriculum. The cooking experiences involve science, measurement, and creative verbal expression. In addition, discussing the history, geography, music and recipes of each country will help enhance the child's vocabulary.

Each country has its own personality. That personality is reflected in the country's language, history, geography, dance, song and foods. A child is deprived of a significant part of education if he is denied the opportunity to obtain knowledge and appreciation of other countries and cultures. This book is designed to aid the teacher in providing a multi-cultural and international approach to education.

Nineteen-eighty-nine and 1990 saw many changes in the world's political scene, especially in the communist countries. In 1990, President George Bush declared the Cold War over. When using the chapters in this book, please take advantage of current periodicals (i.e. news magazines) to get in-depth coverage on worldwide cultural and political issues. Using outside resources with the latest information will make your students aware of the importance of getting to know all of our global neighbors.

SAMPLE LESSON PLAN
INTRODUCING COUNTRIES AROUND THE WORLD

Introduction

This book is designed to help the classroom teacher develop short but informative units about various countries and relate them to the young child. Facts and information about the country and classroom activities are provided in an easy-to-follow format.

Parents will be encouraged to share information about countries that they have visited or to help the child find additional resource materials on the country being studied. The child will be required to return a signed note from his or her parents stating that he or she has permission to sample specific foods as they are introduced in the classroom. The parents may also want to make some of the recipes at home.

Objectives

1. The students will be able to locate the country on the map or globe.
2. The students will be able to color the flag of the country.
3. The students will be able to relate various facts about each country.
4. The students will be able to make and taste a food specific to each country.
5. The students will be able to play a game or engage in an activity related to each country.

Materials

record player and records from the various countries
books about the countries
bulletin boards relating to the countries
maps or globes
artifacts from each country
foods and cooking utensils

Lessons may follow a format similar to the following sample lesson on Mexico

LESSON ONE—MEXICO

Objectives

1. The students will participate in a class discussion about Mexico.
2. Each student will locate three regions in Mexico on a printout sheet.
3. Each student will color the flag of Mexico.

Learning Strategies

1. The teacher becomes familiar with the narrative about Mexico and lists specific information that seems relevant to the children for discussion. Also, before the lesson begins, copies of the map and flag page (page 73) should be made for each child.

2. With the use of a large map of Mexico and a globe, the teacher and students will locate together their home state and then Mexico, so they can get an idea of where Mexico is in relation to where they are.

3. A class discussion follows. The teacher, noting the list of specific information, asks leading questions that encourage children to arrive at the appropriate answers. The following types of questions are given as examples.

    1. Q. *Let's look at the map. There is water on both sides of Mexico. What are the names of these bodies of water?*
       A. *the Pacific Ocean and the Gulf of Mexico.*

    2. Q. *What countries touch Mexico on the map?*
       A. *The United States and Guatemala.*

    3. Q. *Who were the original people who lived in Mexico before Columbus discovered the "New World?"*
       A. *Indians.*

    4. Q. *Mexicans speak Spanish today. Why do you think this is?*
       A. *People from Spain conquered the Indians and brought their own language with them.*

4. Printout sheets of the map and flag are passed out. The teacher will show the students a colored flag of Mexico. They discuss the flag, the Mexican terrain and the three numbered places on the map. They write in the answers that are asked and color the flag.

5. As the children work, the teacher will observe and help individual students.

6. A Mexico center will be set up on a table. Children are asked to contribute to the table any Mexican items that they have at home. (These will be returned when the unit is completed.) Any parents who have a Mexican background are urged to participate in the activities — singing, playing an instrument, teaching a dance, cooking, etc. Items such as a serape, a sombrero, dolls, records, books, pictures by Mexican artists, etc. may be used on the table.

7. Teacher writes vocabulary words on the chalkboard for students to copy.

8. Student's work will be placed on a Mexican bulletin board.

Evaluation

1. The teacher notes the quality of participation in the discussion and in the other activities.

LESSON TWO—30-45 MINUTES

Prior to this day, be sure that parents have been given a note requesting that each child be given permission to sample the foods and requesting a small donation to cover costs.

Objectives

1. The students will make tacos and taste tortillas, enchiladas, refried beans and/or Spanish rice.

Learning Strategies

1. The teacher will tell the students about Mexican family life and the foods of Mexico.
2. The children will get the chance to eat tacos and tortillas.
3. The children will participate in making tacos.

Evaluation

1. Each child gets the chance to taste a tortilla and help make the tacos.

LESSON THREE—30-45 MINUTES

Objectives

1. The children will listen to a Mexican song, *The Mexican Hat Dance.*
2. All the children will play the Mexican game, dancing around the sombrero.
3. The children will make a serape with butcher paper and paints.

Learning Strategies

1. Review the song and movements.
2. To introduce the Mexican Hat Dance, the teacher plays a record of the music or plays it on the piano. Show the children the steps of the dance.
3. Give the children an opportunity to learn to dance the Mexican Hat Dance.

Evaluation

1. The children listen to the song.
2. The teacher observes the students dancing.
3. The children complete their serape.

Numerous other activities can be incorporated into the Lesson Plan. Below are a few examples.*

1) Have the *Greek Olympics.* Play foreign games such as Japanese tag (played similar to our tag except the player must hold the spot where he/she was tagged), Chinese jacks (the jacks are 4 inch pieces of cloth filled with rice and tied), Israeli klass (game like hopscotch except the marker is pushed with a toe while the player hops), or Mexican bola (a 1 foot stick with a paper cup tacked to one end and a 15 inch string with a ball attached tied to the top. You are to try to make the ball land in the cup.)

2) Prepare the recipes contained in each unit at home with the family or at school.

3) Develop language notebooks with the numbers, vocabulary, and derivations of words presented in each chapter.

4) Locate folk stories and folk songs from each country.

5) Make masks with paper mache, tin foil, or construction paper when studying the culture of Mexico, Africa, Indians, and China.

6) Play records or tapes of songs from each country. Try to identify what country the music is from and what instruments are used. (See Bibliography for listings of international songs.)

7) Study the pictures of the dolls presented. Then draw your own ethnic costumes and cut them out for paper doll outfits.

8) Discover and study the heros of the different countries: Martin Luther King, Sun Yat Sin, Pancho Villa.

9) Study the art of each country. Visit museums. Make the art projects presented in each unit and have an art show. For example: Japanese origami and fans, Mexican pottery, Indian batik, American Indian basket weaving, pottery and rug weaving, African wood carving, and Polish paper cuts.

10) Talk with natives of the country and have them visit the class and share their ways of life.

Activities and Resources for Guiding Young Children's Learning. Norma Bernstein Tarrow and Sara Wynn Lundsteen. New York: McGraw Hill, 1981.

Children Around The World

NORTH AMERICA

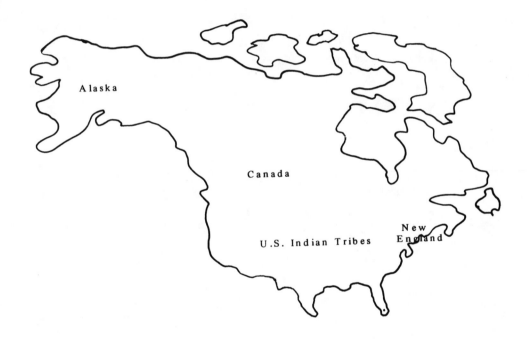

Alaska

Canada

U.S. Indian Tribes

New England

1.

2.

3.

NEW ENGLAND

Color the United States flag.

Can you name these places?

1. _____

2. _____

3. _____

Answers: Maine, Atlantic Ocean, Massachusetts

White stars on a blue background. Alternate red and white stripes.

NEW ENGLAND

The Mayflower, manned by Pilgrims, landed on Plymouth Rock in 1620. Aided by the Indians, the Pilgrims established the Massachusetts Bay Colony and set up their own set of laws.

Many Indians in the New England states helped the Pilgrims—Pequot, Massachuset, Algonquin and Naraganette. The Indians showed the settlers how to plant corn and other vegetables and helped them hunt for game. They taught the Pilgrims to bury fish in each hole that was dug for planting corn to fertilize the poor New England soil. The first Thanksgiving was a celebration held by the Pilgrims and the Indians to give thanks for the blessings they had received.

William Bradford was the first governor of the Massachusetts Bay Colony. Although he provided good leadership, and despite the Indians' help, many colonists died during these first hard winters. People continued to come to America, however, and settlements spread throughout New England and southward until the thirteen original colonies were established: Massachusetts, Connecticut, Rhode Island, New Hampshire, Maryland, New Jersey, Pennsylvania, Delaware, New York, Virginia, North Carolina, South Carolina and Georgia.

People left Europe and came to America for political, religious and economic reasons. For example, Roger Williams established the Baptist colony of Rhode Island because he believed in separation of church and state. America thus became known as the Melting Pot, because people from the other nations of the world came to this free country to worship and live as they wished. England tried to control and exert its authority over the people in the new colonies, however, without granting the colonists certain rights and privileges of British citizenship, such as the right to send a representative to the British Parliament. The colonists cried, "No taxation without representation!" Finally, the repression became unbearable and the people of the new colonies in America revolted.

This American Revolution, known as the War of American Independence in England, began in 1775. New England contributed soldiers and fought on New England soil. The British soldiers were called lobsterbacks because they wore red coats. Two famous battles were the Battle of Lexington and Concord and the Battle of Bunker Hill. The first shot of the American Revolution (known as "the shot that was heard around the world") was fired at Lexington, Massachusetts. Massachusetts celebrates Bunker Hill Day, June 17, in honor of this battle.

The war ended in 1783. The American colonies had won their independence from England.

The New England states began to profit economically and became a competitor of England, producing textile products. Prior to this time, England had a monopoly on the textile industry. Sugar was grown in the Southeast, and rum was distilled in New England and then exchanged for slaves from West Africa.

Locate the states in the United States of America

Color the children of different nationalities.

8

RECIPES

New England Clam Chowder

Fried bacon bits
2 onions, chopped
1 quart shucked clams
6 potatoes
water
salt
pepper
1 can evaporated milk

Fry bacon and add onion. Add clams, potatoes, and water. Boil and simmer until potatoes are soft. Add seasonings and evaporated milk.

Chicken and Noodles

Fryer chicken
Wide egg noodles

Boil chicken in salted water for one hour. Remove and pick meat off the bone. Add noodles to the broth and boil, as directed on package. Add the chicken to the broth.

Pot Roast

Brown both sides of a chuck or rump roast. Arrange peeled carrots, onions and potatoes in the roasting pan. Cook in 350 degree oven for two hours. Add water as needed.

Squash Casserole

summer squash
1 cup sour cream
1 can cream of chicken soup
1 cup grated cheese
½ stick butter

Mix the ingredients together and top with bread crumbs or stuffing mix. Bake in 350 degree oven until hot and bubbly. (Sour cream may be omitted and onions may be added, if desired.)

Potato Salad

Cook potatoes until done in boiling water. Mash potatoes or cut into chunks. Add hard boiled eggs, dill pickles and mayonaise, and stir gently.

Green Bean Casserole

2 cans French style green beans
1 can cream of mushroom soup
1 can cream of onion soup
1 can onion rings

Mix soup and beans. Top with onion rings. Bake in 350 degree oven until hot and bubbly.

The early settlers ate turkey, roast, and other game and meats. They grew fresh vegetables and fixed them in many different ways. The New England settlers also liked baked beans, corn bread and black bread. They drank a lot of coffee and also enjoyed coffee candy and iced coffee.

VOCABULARY

The vocabulary of the new settlers was basically the same as we speak today. However, there were variations in phrases.

Tonic—soda pop
Cobbler—shoe repairman
Down cellar—basement
Cruller—long twisted pastry
Moxie—soda pop that tastes like bitter root beer
New England boiled dinner—corned beef, cabbage, beets, carrots and potatos cooked in the same pot. (The corned beef should be cooked about one hour before adding the vegetables.)

AMERICAN INDIAN TRIBES

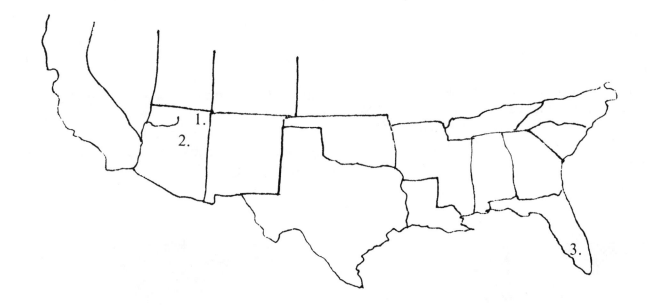

Color the Indian Symbols

Can you find these Indian tribes?

1. _____.
2. _____.
3. _____.

Answers: Navajo, Hopi, Miccosukee

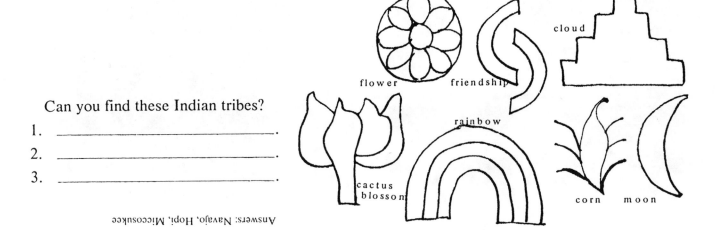

flower friendship cloud

cactus blosson rainbow corn moon

INDIAN TRIBES OF NORTH AMERICA

The Miccosukee Indians have lived in the Everglades of South Florida since before Florida was admitted to the Union. In 1962, the U.S. government officially recognized the Miccosukee Tribe. The Indians now have schools, a library, a police force and Tribal officers. Miccosukees speak both their native language and English. Some favorite foods are fried bread, sofkie, hamburgers and cokes. Tradition is strong with the Miccosukees. For instance, they still use their traditional language, medicine, clan system and rituals. Traditional patchwork designs are found on many of their handmade clothes. Miccosukees live in a village, an example of a real family "camp." Many live in *chickees*, hut-type homes. In each village; sleeping and working chickees are arranged around the central cooking chickee and its symbolic star-shaped fire. The camp traditionally belonged to the clan matriarch. A young man would have to set up a sleeping chickee in the camp if he wanted to marry a daughter of the clan.

The Navajo, numbering about 80,000, is the largest tribe in the United States. Their reservations are predominantly located in New Mexico and Arizona. They were semi-nomadic herders of sheep. They became known for the blankets and rugs they made from the wool of their sheep. This craft is valued highly today. The geometric designs and other designs the Navajo use in their craft are so distinctive and well established that they have acquired names. For coloring, they use numerous dyes in their blankets including dye baths from berries, roots, flowers and bark.

The Hopi Tribe, numbering about 6,500, is located in Arizona. They are known for the Kachina Dolls (See next page.) They also make beautiful wicker bowls and baskets. The Hopi pottery is sold for decoration as well as for cooking. Hopi also work in silver. Their silverwork was encouraged by the Museum of Northern Arizona and they developed a unique style in their silverwork based on their pottery designs.

Miccosukee Indian Doll

INDIAN ARTIFACTS

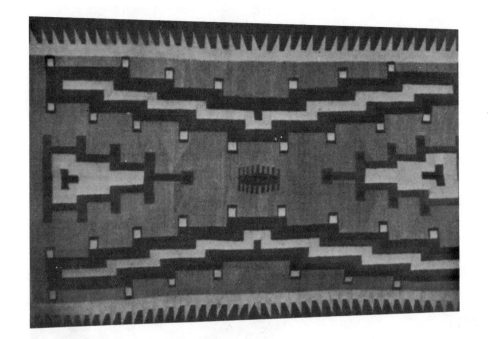

Navajo Indian Rug—Grey Mountain Rug Design. Given to author's family by Indian Chief in Albuquerque, New Mexico over 50 years ago.

Hopi Kachina Witch Doctor

The painted wooden dolls represent masked dancers, who represent *kachinas*. Kachinas are religious figures in the Hopi religion and are similar to the Christian saints. They serve as go-betweens for mortals and the more important deities. The dolls themselves are not idols and are not worshipped or prayed to. They are used in the religious training of the young people to teach them the characteristics and names of the more than two hundred kachinas which they will see during their lifetime. The children receive the dolls as gifts during kachina ceremonies. The Hopi men carve the dolls from the root of the cottonwood tree.

For further information:
SOUTHWESTERN INDIAN ARTS & CRAFTS. K.C. Publications, P.O. Box 14883, Las Vegas. Nev. 89114.

15

CLASSROOM ART ACTIVITIES

The Indian maiden puppet is made from two paper plates connected with a brad. Make arms and legs from construction paper and glue them in the proper place. Use felt, yarn braids, and paint to add to the creativity of the puppet.

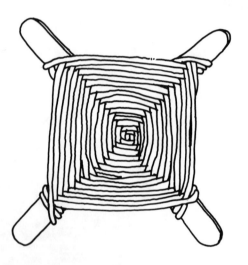

The God's Eye is made with two crossed sticks and yarn. The yarn is wrapped around one stick and brought over to the next stick. The process is repeated until the sticks are almost completely covered.

Indian pottery can be made from playdough, modeling clay or ceramic clay—whatever is available. The coil pot is shown. Roll snake-like "ropes" of clay and mount them on top of one another to form the pots.

INDIAN RECIPES

Fry Bread

2 cups self-rising flour
Add enough milk or water to make a good consistency
Pat a handful of dough flat
Fry in deep fat until light brown

Eat it plain or with butter or honey. You may want to dip it in hot chili.

Indian Pudding

5 cups milk
⅔ cup molasses
½ cup yellow corn meal
¼ cup sugar
dash of cinnamon, nutmeg, allspice, ginger and salt
2 tsp. butter

Scald 4 cups milk. Stir in other ingredients. Cook over low heat about 10 minutes until the mixture thickens. Pour into 2 quart baking dish. Pour remaining milk on top and bake in 300 degree oven for 3 hours. Serve warm or chilled with milk or ice cream.

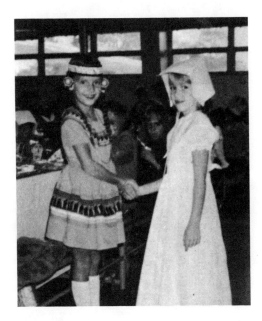

VOCABULARY

Miccosukee

Breakfast—*Hampole Empeeke*
Lunch—*Empekchoobe*
Dinner—*Oopyah-empeeke*
Side orders—*Empeeke Alahkeeka*
Desserts—*Empek Kamoshke*
Beverages—*Empeeke Shachaakahshkeeke*
Tribe chairman—*leader or chief*
Basket—*shanche*
Beads—*naakaashe*
Doll—*yaataabe*

Navajo

one—*3ááii*
two—*naaki*
three—*táá*
four—*dii*
five—*ashdia*
six—*hastáa*
seven—*tsostsid*
eight—*tseebii*
nine—*nahast ei*
ten—*neeznaa*

Are you hungry?
Dichinish nilt?

Do you want something?
T'áadoo le'ésh ninizin?

Do you understand me?
Da' shidinits'a' ásh?

American Indian Words

teepee
wigwam
raccoon
tomahawk
caribou
chipmunk

ALASKA

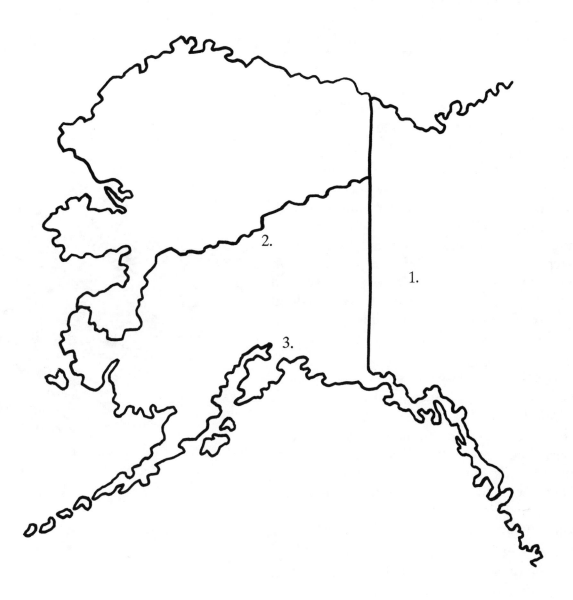

Can you name these places?

1. _____.

2. _____.

3. _____.

ALASKA

Eskimos live in Alaska near the North Pole. A few families usually live in small villages which are separated by vast distances. Their permanent homes are made of whale bone ribs and sod. Eskimos also build temporary homes of ice, called igloos, when they are on long hunting trips. They also use ice for water and wind breaks. Since the temperature in winter in Alaska is often 30 degrees below zero, water freezes almost instantly. To get water, an Eskimo must chip ice from an ice block and quickly take it inside.

Fishing is a means of survival for the Eskimo. A family and its dogs need approximately forty to fifty pounds of fish per day. When large bodies of water are frozen over, Eskimos fish through fishing holes they dig in the ice. Sometimes they have to dig as deeply as four feet into the ice to reach unfrozen water. All Eskimos do not fish in this manner, however. Some live inland and fish in streams. After fish are caught, they are dried and used for food during the winter.

Hunting is also a means of survival for the Eskimo. The Eskimo uses the meat of seals for food and the seal's skin for making *kayaks* (canoes). Blubber is melted into sea oil and is a main source of vitamins. Eskimos also hunt the walrus for its meat and its skin which can be made into boots. The ivory tusks are carved and sold for needed goods. Some Eskimos are primarily reindeer herders and the reindeer is their major source of food and clothing. The Eskimos follow reindeer wherever they roam, building temporary homes as they go.

Many Eskimos become lost while hunting and fishing. It is customary for the family members to hang their boots on a rafter in the home. As long as the boots swing, there is hope that the missing family member will return.

Eskimo families are very close. Their lifestyle evolves around the home. Babies are treated well because Eskimos believe that the souls of ancestors return in the form of infants.

The Eskimo culture has many legends which are reflected in their dances and festivals.

Children also engage in activities such as piggy back races and the blanket toss game. The blanket toss game is similar to our trampoline. A walrus skin is held tightly and tossed as someone jumps on it. The Eskimos' custom of kissing is different from ours—they rub noses!

ESKIMO FOLK SONG

The majority of the commentary on Eskimo music before 1900 was steeped in cultural bias and aesthetic prejudice. Studies by Frazs Boas, Zygmunt Estreicher, Helen H. Roberts and Bruno Nettls of Eskimo music have shown that the folk art expression of the Eskimo music is a highly integrated and complex art form. Their melodies are complex and varied and the rhythms are expressive and interesting. The dances of the Eskimos vary. They range from the solo dances of the Caribou Eskimo, which involve very little bodily movement (only a few steps forward and backward), to wild round dances with torches by the Eskimos of Alaska.

AJAAJ—*Drum Song*

A n aa jaaa ha-jee an-o aa kee-a-gi-a-
Ah, Ah, you've come back; You were once filled with furious

nee nuaa-ni ta-taa-jaja-aj-jaa-jaa
rage, You were once coward and a-fraid to fight.

a-ja-ay–oo–jaa–jaa-jee a n aa ja-aa ha-jee
Have you—come back—at last To—seek—vengence?

a-o-aa taa wa aa te-nu-at taa—
Wretch-ed fool! ride—your broken pu-ny sled

ja jaaj-jaa jaa a-ja-aj—oo.
For the fight; beat drums! I am read-y, oh!

CLASSROOM ACTIVITY
Make a sugar cube igloo.

RECIPES

Baked Fish
Butter
Fish fillet (whatever is in season)
lemon
salt, pepper
paprika
bread crumbs

Place the fillets in a baking dish. Sprinkle with salt, pepper, paprika and lemon juice. Sprinkle the bread crumbs over the fish. Bake in the oven at 350 degrees for 30 minutes.

Baked Alaska

Use a spongecake or yellow cake for a base. Pile ice cream on top, leaving about ½ inch free around the edge. Cover with meringue. Prepare meringue by beating four or more egg whites with an electric mixer until they stand in peaks. Cover the ice cream with the meringue and bake at 500 degrees for 4 or 5 minutes.

VOCABULARY

kayak—boats made from seal skin
igloo—house made of ice
komatiks—sleds pulled by dogs

CANADA

Color the Canadian flag.

Can you name these places?

1. _____ .
2. _____ .
3. _____ .

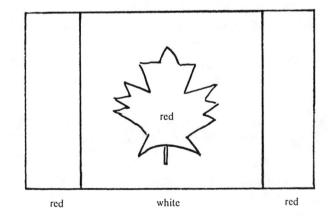

red   white   red

23

CANADA

Canada is the second largest country in the world, slightly larger than Europe in land area and 176,000 square miles larger than the United States. Canada, however, has only one-tenth the population of the U.S. Most sections of the northern part of Canada are frozen wasteland, so most Canadians live in the South. Almost all areas of Canada, however, have cold winters. More than two thirds of the country has an average January temperature below zero degrees fahrenheit.

Canada has seven geographic or land regions: 1) the Appalachian region; 2) the St. Lawrence Lower Great Lakes Lowlands; 3) the Canadian Shield; 4) the Hudson Bay Lowlands; 5)the Western Interior Plains; 6) the Western Mountain region; and 7) the Artic Islands.

The government of Canada is parliamentary. The legislature is known as the House of Commons. Canada's prime minister is the country's leader. He chooses a cabinet of ministers to help him govern. Canada is divided into *provinces*, similar to the states of the United States, and *territories*, geographical areas generally less populated than the provinces. The ten provinces of Canada are: 1) Alberta; 2) British Columbia; 3) Manitoba; 4) New Brunswick; 5) Newfoundland; 6) Nova Scotia; 7) Ontario; 8) Prince Edward Island; 9) Quebec; and 10) Saskatchewan. The two territories are the Northwest and the Yukon territories. Each province has its own legislature and the territories are governed by councils.

Most Canadians can trace their ancestry to Europe, primarily England and France. The two official languages of the country are English and French. Most French Canadians live in the province of Quebec. Many Scots live in Nova Scotia and Prince Edward Island. Many Canadians of British descent live in New Brunswick and southern Ontario. Indians and Eskimos also live in both the territories and provinces of Canada.

Each of Canada's provinces has its own school system. In all provinces except Quebec, school is taught in English and resembles the schools of the U.S. Most Canadian schools are coed and have eight elementary grades and four high school grades. Usually a Canadian student goes to college for three years to obtain a B.A. degree. Some majors, however, require an additional degree. Religious schools also exist in Canada and are supported by public funds. Protestant and Catholic religions are the predominant religions in Canada, although members of other religions live there also.

Canadians live very much like Americans do. Some major exceptions are the French Canadians in Quebec, who speak French instead of English, and the Eskimos, who make their living by hunting, fishing, selling furs, or working in mining camps. Eskimos also ride in boats called *kayaks*, made from animal skins, and travel across the snow on *komatiks*, sleds pulled by dogs.

CANADIAN GAMES

Canadian sports and games had their beginnings in England, Scotland, and France. Hockey is the national game of Canada. Children play in leagues in the winter. Children learn to skate and to ski at very early ages. Tobogganing and dog sled racing are also popular in winter. Indoor games include follow-the-leader, hide the object, hopscotch, spin the plate and tag. Summer activities include canoe riding, soccer, fishing, football, golf, hiking, horseback riding, swimming, and tennis. Young Eskimo boys practice rowing kayaks to get ready for seal hunts when they are older.

French-Canadian Song

ALOUETTE

A-lou-et-te, gen-tille A-lou-et-te, A-lou-et-te, Je te plu-me-rai.

Je te plu-me-rai la tête, Je te plu-me-rai la tête, à la téte, à la tête. Oh!

A-lou-et-te, gen-tille A-lou-et-te, A-lou-et-te, Je te plu-me-rai.

Je te plu-me-rai le bec, Je te plu-me- rai le bec, à le bec, à le bec.

à la tête, à la tête.

A-lou-ette, A-lou-ette. Oh!

RECIPES

Pate Brisee*

1½ C. flour
dash salt
8 T. unsalted butter, cut into ½" pieces
4–6 T. ice water

Mix flour and salt in medium-sized bowl. Cut in butter a piece at a time until mixture resembles coarse meal. Stir in water, 1 T. at a time, until mixture cleans side of bowl. Press dough gently into balls with hands. Wrap in plastic. Refrigerate 30 minutes.

Cheese Barquettes Alsacienne

Pate Brisee (½ recipe given above)
1½ T. unsalted butter
¾ C. chopped onion
2 t. flour
2 eggs
¼ C. heavy cream
½ t. Dijon mustard
¼ t. salt
⅛ t. white pepper
dash nutmeg
⅓ C. shredded Swiss Gruyere cheese

Roll out Pate Brisee on floured surface into 12" square. Cut dough into 8 ovals ½" larger than barquette pans. Press lightly into pans and place in freezer until firm—about 5 minutes. Heat oven to 375 degrees. Place barquette pan on baking sheet and bake 5 minutes. Pierce bubbles which form, to release steam and bake 5 minutes longer. Remove pastry from pans while still warm and let cool completely on wire racks.

Melt butter in skillet over medium heat. Add onion and saute. Stir in flour and cook, stirring constantly, about 1 minute. Add cheese, a little at a time, and continue cooking until cheese melts, stirring constantly. Separately, beat eggs. Combine eggs with cream, mustard, salt, pepper and nutmeg and blend well. Stir in the cheese and onion mixture and blend well. Heat oven to 375 degrees. Place barquette pastry shells on baking sheet and fill with mixture. Bake until golden brown, approximately 15 minutes. Serve warm.

Snow Ice Cream With Maple Topping

* The maple tree is a symbol of Canada and maple syrup is very popular in Canada.

1 C. ice cream or snow
maple syrup

Heat syrup and pour over the ice cream or snow. Serve in bowls.

ASIA & THE SOUTH PACIFIC

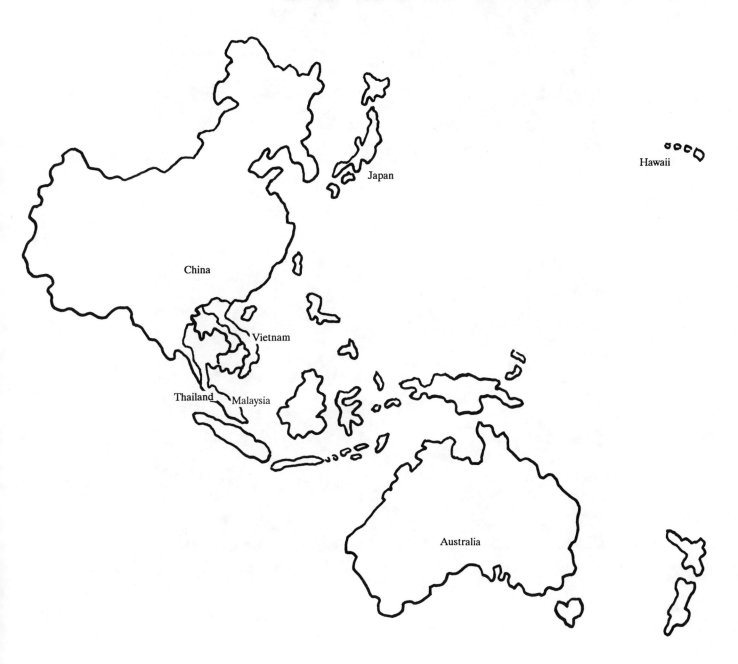

Hawaii

Japan

China

Vietnam

Thailand Malaysia

Australia

27

Chinese commune children dancing for visitors.   Photo by Alma David

Children's dance in China.   Photo by Alma David

CHINA

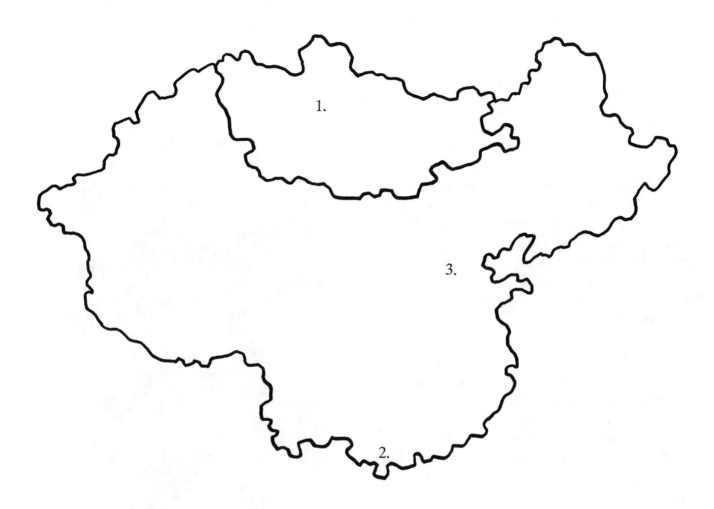

1.

3.

2.

Can you name these places?

1. _____ .
2. _____ .
3. _____ .

Answers: Mongolia, Hong Kong, Peking

Color the Chinese flag.

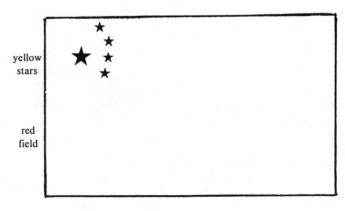

yellow
stars

red
field

CHINA

The official name of China is the Republic of China. The Chinese capital is Beijing, formerly Peking. Located in Eastern Asia, China is the world's third largest country in land area. It also has more than one-fifth of the world's population.

China has eighteen provinces. The waterways that bound China are the Yellow Sea, the East China Sea and the South China Sea.

China's time is fifteen hours ahead of the United States Eastern Standard Time. Geographically, China extends farther to the north and to the south than does the United States. Therefore, the weather in parts of China is similar to that in the United States. In the northern part of China, however, Siberian winds are powerful and cold in the winter - colder than what we experience in the United States.

Eighty percent of the Chinese people are farmers. Therefore the Chinese economy relies heavily on agriculture.

The Chinese people celebrate two major holidays each year: the Spring Festival and the New Year. October 1 is the Chinese New Year. October 1 is the anniversary of the founding of the Chinese People's Republic in 1949. Each year parades are held to celebrate the New Year.

The Chinese language is one of the world's oldest languages. It is spoken in many different dialects. In all, over 800,000,000 people speak Chinese. Chinese is, however, one of mankind's most difficult languages to read. Traditional written Chinese consists of many *characters,* each of which represents a separate word or idea, rather than letters. In traditional Chinese a person must be able to recognize over 3,500 characters before he can read a novel, and over 10,000 characters before he can read a classical Chinese work. Because of the great difficulty involved in learning to read traditional Chinese, in 1950 the Communist government introduced the Chinese alphabet to simplify the written language.

Since 1950 the population's literacy rate has improved in China. Children attend primary school for five to six years and middle school

three years. The curriculum consists of Chinese, geography, music and arithmetic. The secondary schools are work-study schools and the students' work helps support the school. The subjects taught include science, literature and mathematics. Chinese children start learning English at about the seventh grade level.

CHINESE CHECKERS

Two to six players
Board made of cardboard or soft wood
Discs or marbles

The game is played on a six-pointed star, as shown. Use a commercially made board or make your own. If you make your own, paint each point of the star a different color and then shellac the entire board. If the board is flat, use discs as "men." If holes are bored in the wood, use marbles. Each player uses ten men. The men are placed on the star point beginning with the point, as shown. Each player tries to get all his men across the board to fill in the opposite star point. He may move in any direction except backward, one place at a time. A man may "jump" over another man, and can even make a series of continuous jumps, in one move. The men he jumps over, however, are not removed from the board as in American checkers. The first player to fill in the opposite star point with his men wins.

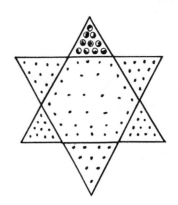

DRAW A CHINESE CHARACTER

Using a pen or pencil, follow the diagram to correctly draw the Chinese character for "sky."

Chinese children

Photo by Alma David.

31

RECIPES

Chinese seasonings frequently consist of the following: salt, pepper, sugar and sesame oil. Wine, vinegar, cornstarch and frying oil are also used.

Chinese cooking instruments include the following: cleavers, chopping block, spatula, strainers, wok, and steamers.

Egg Flower Soup*

3 C. clear canned chicken broth
dash salt
chopped scallion
1 T. cornstarch
2 T. water
1 egg, beaten

Bring chicken broth to a boil. Separately, add water slowly to the cornstarch. Add cornstarch liquid to the broth. Stir until it begins to thicken and becomes clear. Add salt. Pour the beaten egg into the broth and continue to cook. It will cook quickly. Top with scallion.

Sweet and Sour Pork

1 lb. pork loin, cut up
1 T. soy sauce
1 egg yolk
7–8 T. cornstarch
1 C. pickled relish
1 green pepper
dash garlic
6 C. oil
3 T. vinegar
3 T. sugar
3 T. water
3 T. ketsup
dash salt
1½ t. water

Soak cut up pieces of pork in soy sauce, egg yolk and 1 T. cornstarch. Mix with 6 more T. of cornstarch and fry for 3 minutes. Remove from pan. Reheat pan and stir-fry green pepper, garlic and salad. Add vineger, sugar, water, ketsup and salt. Add 1 more t. of cornstarch and water to thicken. Pour mixture over pork and serve.

Stir-Fried Shrimp with Garlic

1 lb. fresh shrimp
½ T. cornstarch
oil
dash of salt
2 T. chopped garlic
½ T. chopped hot red pepper (optional)

Boil shrimp in pan of water for 3 minutes until bright pink in color. Remove, devein and mix with cornstarch. Stir-fry shrimp, garlic and seasonings.

VOCABULARY

The Chinese people have a special way of writing. They use characters made up of brush or pen strokes which give readers *ideas* of what is meant and *pictures* of words. These are called ideographs and pictographs. Special sounds are made to match each picture or idea.

姨	aunt
疫	sickness
醫	doctor
億	100,000,000
怡	(was) joyful
外	foreign
界	wonderful
亦	how

JAPAN

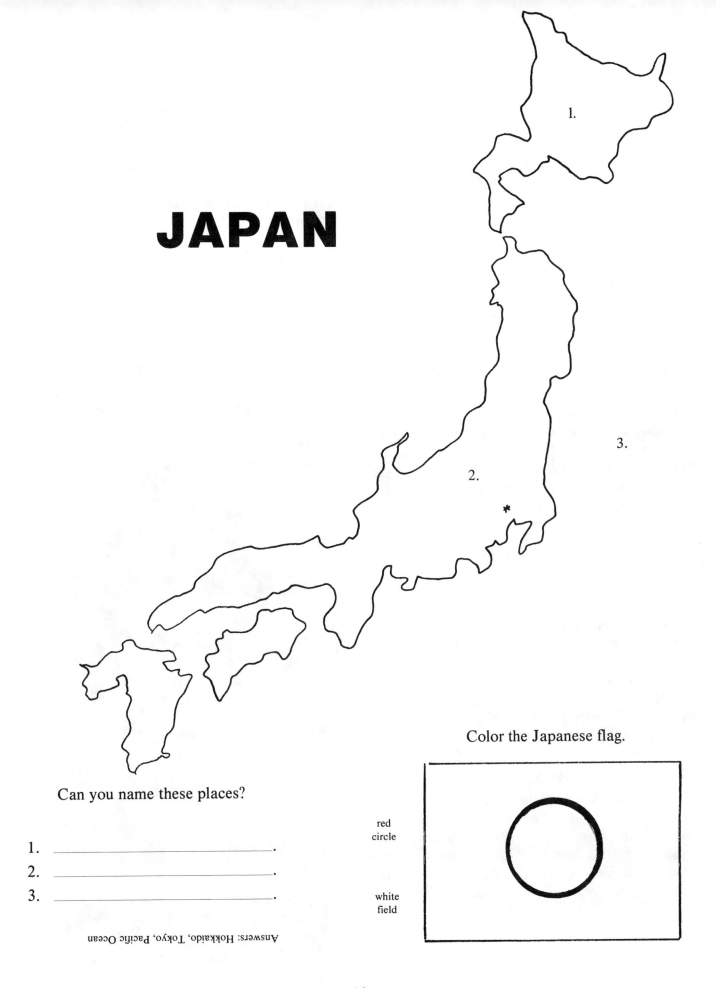

1.

2.

3.

*

Can you name these places?

1. _____ .
2. _____ .
3. _____ .

Answers: Hokkaido, Tokyo, Pacific Ocean

Color the Japanese flag.

red circle

white field

33

JAPAN

The Japanese people call their country *Nippon* or *Nihon*, which means *origin of the sun*. The country's flag represents this concept. It contains a single red ball on a white background. The Japanese heritage is full of similar legends and symbols.

Japan's four islands cover about the same land area as California and its population density is one of the highest in the world. Japan has over 124 million inhabitants.

Japan has a very diversified climate. In Hokkaido the snow is heavy in winter, while in Kyushu people are able to bathe in outdoor springs during the winter months. There are many earthquakes in Japan; however, few of them cause damage.

Japanese farmland is poor, but Japanese farmers grow rice, tea and vegetables by means of careful cultivation. The Japanese produce charcoal and wood from their forests. Fishing is also an important industry. Japan's waterfalls are a source of hydro-electric power. Japan is a world leader in the electronics industry.

Japan is a democratic country. The electorate or voting population is known as the Japanese National Diet. The Japanese government is composed of an Emperor, a Prime Minister, the House of Councillors and the House of Representatives. The House of Representatives is similar to America's Congress and is divided into a Senate and a House. The Prime Minister is elected by the Diet. His election is then approved by the Emperor. The Emperor also approves the Chief Justice of the Supreme Court, receives foreign dignitaries and hosts ceremonial functions. In Japan the voting age is twenty.

Japan's literacy rate of 95% is one of the highest in the world. Children attend elementary school for six years and junior high for three years. Students must pass strict entrance examinations to be able to attend the three-year high schools, colleges and universities.

The arts of Japan are beautiful and expressive. For example, the popular Haiku form of poetry is a Japanese creation. A Haiku is a three-lined poem of seventeen syllables, usually arranged in a five—seven—five pattern. Another Japanese art is Ikebana flower arranging. In an Ikebana flower arrangement, the tallest or highest flowers represent heaven; middle flowers represent man; and the lower flowers represent earth. Another example of the Japanese arts is Sumi-e painting. Sumi-e painting is one of the greatest traditions of Far Eastern art. It is done with black ink on paper that is white, pure and clean. The artist leaves the white background untouched—he draws in no shading to suggest three dimensions. The white areas give the painting spatial depth. The artist Tenkei Tachibana, whose royal family association name is Yoshihito Yozen, is a world renowned Sumi-e expert.

ORIGAMI

Origami is the Japanese art of paper folding. Origami has been practiced in Japan for over a thousand years by adults and children alike. The only material needed is paper. Most of the time colored paper about four to six inches square is used. Two sheets of different colored paper may be used by placing them back to back. The four basic rules of Origami are:

1. Choose a flat, hard surface as your place of work.

2. Be sure to make your folds straight.

3. Make your creases sharp by pressing with your thumbnail.

4. Choose paper with color, texture and design that will add beauty to the piece. Experiment with different kinds of paper: onion skin, gift wrapping, comic strips, and others.

Origami books may be purchased at many bookstores. Try to follow the directions below for making a hat:

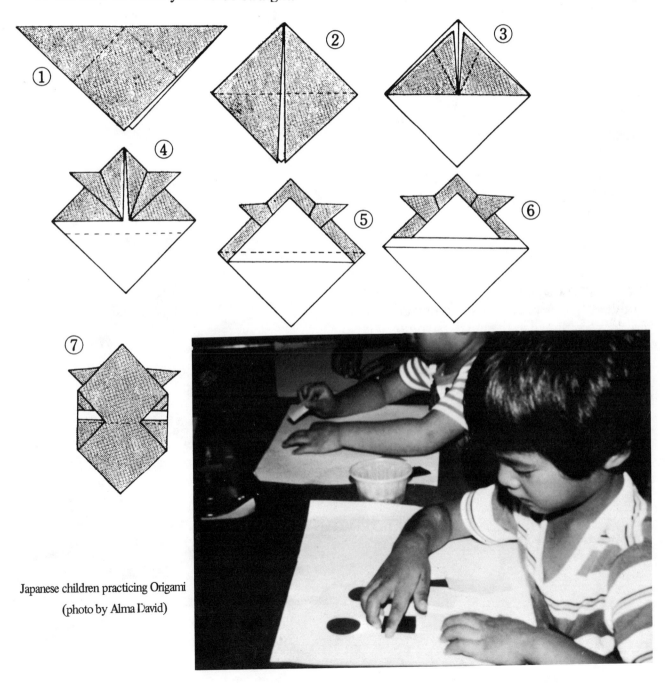

Japanese children practicing Origami
(photo by Alma David)

35

RECIPES

Teriyaki Chicken

¼ C. soy sauce
1 package deboned chicken breasts, cut into pieces
1 C. mushrooms
1 C. chopped onions
1 C. bean sprouts (optional)
oil

Marinate the chicken pieces in soy sauce overnight, if possible.

Saute chicken in oil until brown. Add onion, mushrooms and soy sauce.   Heat thoroughly. Add   bean sprouts. Serve with cooked rice.

This recipe can also be used with flank steak.

Fried Rice

left over meat or poultry scraps (spam, ham, chicken, etc.)
2–3 eggs
½ t. salt
⅓ C. oil
4 C. cooked rice
1 C. bean sprouts
2 T. minced onion
1 t. Chinese brown gravy syrup or soy sauce

Brown onion in oil. Add leftover meat. Separately, scramble egg. Add egg, bean sprouts, rice, then gravy or soy sauce to the meat and onions. Heat until steaming.

You may want to try eating with chopsticks.

VOCABULARY

one—*ichi*
two—*ni*
three—*san*
four—*shi*
five—*go*
six—*roku*
seven—*nana*
eight—*hachi*
nine—*kyuh*
ten—*juh*

friend—*tomodachi*
school—*gakko*
car—*kuruma*
home—*katei*
name—*na*

Buddhism is the major religion of Japan

THAILAND

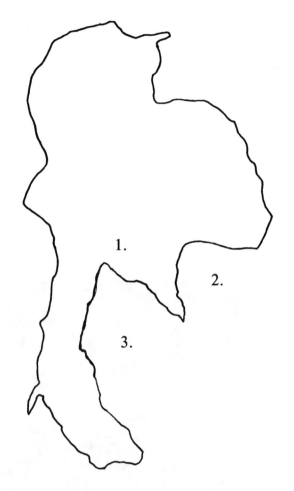

1.

2.

3.

Can you name these places?

1. _____ .
2. _____ .
3. _____ .

Color the Thai flag.

red	
white	
blue	
white	
red	

37

THAILAND

Thailand, known as Siam for many years, is located on the Indo-Chinese Peninsula in Southeast Asia. It is surrounded by Burma, Laos, Vietnam, Cambodia and Malaysia and it borders the Gulf of Thailand. The Thai people originally came from southeastern China.

Monarchs played an important role in shaping Thailand's destiny. The present king's ancestor, King Mongkut (Rama IV), was an intellectual and a scholar. He studied a variety of subjects, including astronomy and geography, and played a major role in the modernization of Siam by minting currency, constructing canals and roads, and printing a newspaper. In 1862, Anna Leonowens left England and went to Thailand to tutor King Rama's eighty-two children at the royal palace. The book "Anna and the King of Siam" and the movie "The King and I" are based on her experiences.

In 1932, a group of young Thais who had acquired knowledge of the democratic form of government through studies at American and European universities, instigated a bloodless coup and forced King Rama VII to sign a constitution which created a constitutional monarchy. In 1939, Siam became a democratic country, and its name was changed to Thailand, "Land of the Free." The present constitution provides for a king as chief of state, a council of ministers which has executive power and is headed by a prime minister, a National Assembly which has legislative power, and the Court of Justice which has judicial power.

Schools are important in Thailand. The schools' curricula are designed to stress the country's history, math, geography, science, philosophy, legends and Buddhism. Students learn English as a second language.

The Thais are renowned for their artistic abilities. They weave baskets, mats, brocades and silk and they make beautiful objects out of gems and silver. Thailand has an elegant National Theater where centuries-old legends are acted out in beautiful costumes. The Thai's primary musical instruments are gongs, xylophones, cymbals and drums.

Favorite sports in Thailand are volleyball and ball games that are similar to soccer. Children also enjoy jacks, kite flying, hopscotch and marbles.

Important industries in Thailand are automobile assembly, electrical goods and textiles. Major minerals mined in Thailand are gas, antimony, iron, manganese and tungsten.

THAI PROVERBS AND CUSTOMS

The customs and beliefs in Thailand are quite different from those in America. Here are some examples:

The Thai believe that the head is the home of the soul. It is sacred and should not be touched.

The feet are the least sacred part of the body. It would be an insult to point at anything with your feet or to cross your legs in front of elders.

Women must never touch a Buddhist monk or offer to shake his hand.

It is improper for men and women to touch each other in public.

Thai always speak quietly.

Thai always take their shoes off when entering a home or temple.

Here are some Thai proverbs, translated into English:

If you receive a quarter, save a dime; your savings will grow to a dollar in time. Be thrifty, but buy those things you need. If your quarters are few, when you spend, take heed.

Return bad deeds with good deeds, selfishness with giving, hatred with love and kind wishes.

If you want to choose an elephant, look at its tail,
If you want to choose a girl, look at her mother,
To be more certain, look at her grandmother.

Think of your own proverbs.

Thai school children

39

RECIPES

Peanut Sauce*

1 t. lemon juice
1 onion, minced
salt
1 t. dried red pepper leaves
1 t. brown sugar
1 t. soy sauce
1 C. oven-heated ground peanuts

Mix and cook until heated.

Serve with flank steak that has been marinated in soy sauce and cooked on bamboo skewers.

Lumpia

2 T. water
1 C. flour
1 t. cornstarch
dash salt

Roll on skillet, like a pancake. Brush with oil. Blot. Add a mixture of ground beef, onion, celery, pork, or other leftover meat. Fry.

Satay (sates)

Marinate beef, pork, chicken or shrimp in soy sauce, lime juice and garlic. Place thin strips on bamboo skewers. Cook on a hibachi or in a broiler. Dip into a sauce of ketsup, vinegar, sugar and water or peanut sauce.

VOCABULARY

The Thai language has 44 consonants and 32 vowels with 5 tones. A word pronounced in different tones will mean different things.

khun kreo—teacher
mug rian—students
rong rian—school
dek poo ying—girl
dek poo chai—boy
Sa wad dee—Greetings
mah (common tone)—to come
mah (high tone)—a horse
mah (rising tone)—a dog

THE THAI NATIONAL ANTHEM
(Phonetic Spelling)

Prathte...thai, ruam leu—at neu—ah chart chur—ah Thai...pen pracha—raj... patai khong.

Thai took su—an, yoo damrong kong wai... dai tang mu—an duey Thai lu—an...mai... raksa

Mak...kee, Thai nee rak saghob tae thung rob mai klard, ekkaraj...cha mai hai krai kom...

Kee...sala...leu—at took yard pen chart plee...ta—lerng pratate chart Thai tawee mee chai chajo'

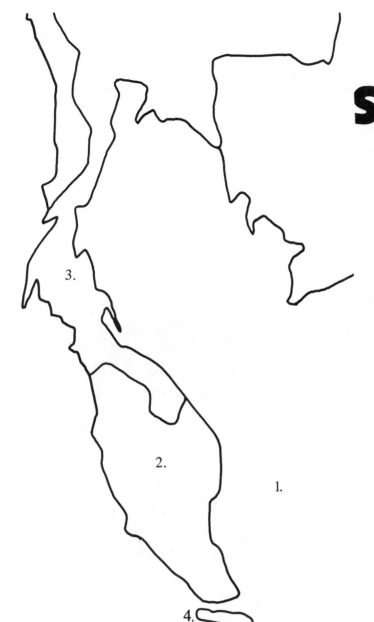

SINGAPORE and MALAYSIA

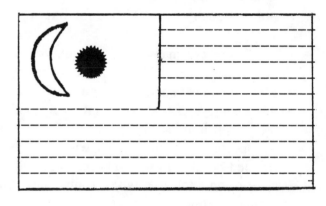

Color the Malaysian flag
Red,white stripes
Yellow moon,star on blue background

Can you name these places?

1. _____.
2. _____.
3. _____.
4. _____.

Red,
white stars-moon

White

Color the Singapore flag.

SINGAPORE and MALAYSIA

Singapore, the City of the Lions, is an island of 618.1 square kilometers standing at the crossroads of Southeast Asia. It is a most forward thinking and progressive commercial and industrial center supported by excellent modern facilities. This intriguing island republic maintains a unique combination of past British tradition and modern growth. It is the second busiest port in the world. Singapore was only a fishing village when Sir Stanford Raffles of the British East India Company landed there in 1819 and made it a British maritime base. In 1957 full international self-government was achieved. After 140 years of British rule, 3 years of Japanese and 2 years within the Malaysia Federation, Singapore was separated from Malaysia and became a fully independent sovereign nation on August 9, 1965. A quality environment is maintained in Singapore with strict environmental policies such as a $500 fine for littering.

There are many different cultures living in Singapore. China Town, Little India and Arab Street demonstrate the local cultural diversity of this country. Local merchants sell goods from their shop houses. People travel in all types of transportation from the old tri-shaws (bicycles pedaled by drivers with a basket attached for the rider-often a tourist), buses, trains, and excellent modern airline.

Malaysia, a country just north of Singapore, offers views of palaces, plantations, villages where handicrafts are demonstrated, beautiful beaches and exquisite mosques and temples. Rubber plantations, as well as coconut, coco, palm oil, banana, pineapple and coffee provide much of the economy of Malaysia.

The palace Instana Besar houses many royal artifacts. Many people in Malaysia, as well as Singapore, are Moslems. Moslems believe in five vows: worship one God, pray five times daily, visit Mecca (their Holy City in Saudi Arabia), give alms to the poor, and fast 40 days a year.

Moslems are wrapped in white cloth and buried without a coffin lying on their side facing Mecca.

Many soldiers died during World War II during the Japanese invasion of Singapore and Malaysia. Over 24,000 soldiers and airman of many races united in service to the British crown are buried in a memorial cemetary on the Singapore-Malaysia border.

EDUCATION IN
SINGAPORE AND MALAYSIA

The schools in Singapore have adequate, but by American standards, uncomfortable facilities and limited materials. Most teachers are young women who lecture in front of classes. Uniforms are the common dress. Religious schools are available. Students attend public or private schools. Religious ethnic foods of the students are offered in the school cafeteria because certain religions believe in eating or not eating certain foods. English is the primary language in Singapore, but Malay is also taught. Although school isn't compulsory, 97% do attend. Kindergarten is available for ages four to six; primary attendance for four years, then an exam is required prior to high school. An exit exam is also required after two years of high school before university acceptance.

In Malaysia, school attendance isn't compulsory but most attend the free schools for six years of primary school, one year of English and Malay, then five years of secondary school. Two years of pre-university work are required prior to university attendance. There are five universities and six colleges in Malaysia. The elementary curriculum includes physical education, religion, and cultural heritage and dance. Many schools separate the boys from the girls, since Buddhist monks teach some classes and they are not allowed to come in close contact with girls.

RECIPES

There is such a variety of foods in Singapore that it is difficult to pick a single recipe. It is a mixture of foods brought from China, Malaysia and India mixed with local variations and the food from the West.

Sample these fruits, if available. Some are not available in the US-why not?

pineapple
starfruit
mangosteen
nangka
papaya
duku
chiker
jambu-air
mango
rambutan

Some favorite Chinese foods follow. Order the food at a Chinese Restrauant or find the recipe in a Chinese cookbook.

Hokkien cuisine favorite: Hokkein mee (noodles) a mixture of thick yellow noodles and rice vermicelli (bee hoon) cooked with prawns, squid, beansprouts and a touch of lime and red chilies.

Hakka cuisine favorite: Stewed pig's trotters and Yong Tau Foo, a fish ball recipe

Szechuan cuisine favorite: Diced chicken with dried chilies (often spicy hot food)

Peking cuisine favorite: Peking Duck

Some favorite Malay foods: Satay, skewers of seasoned chicken beef mutton grilled over charcoal, served on a bed of cool sliced cucumber and onion with a bowl of spicy peanut gravy

Ketupat: Small rice cake

Sotoayam; Spiced chicken broth filled with beansprouts, rice cake chunks, shreds of chicken

Tofu dishes: Tofu is a flat solid chunk of beancurd

Prata dishes: light flaky Indian Pancakes

Pra kosong: Prata served with a bowl of thin curry gravy

Murtabak: Prata filled with mutton and onion

Seafood, especially prawns and squid, as well as a wide varity of Japanese foods such as sushi (balls of vinegared rice topped with seafood) and sukiyaki (thinly sliced beef and vegetables cooked in a pan) are also very popular in Singapore and Malaysia.

VOCABULARY

The people of Singapore speak English but also learn Malay. The people in Malaysia speak Malay but also learn English.

1 E
2 R
3 Sun
4 Phsi
5 Oo
6 Lu
7 Se
8 BA
9 CHU
10 Shi

Malay language uses the Roman letters as does English but the different order and sounds make it unrecognizable.

Hasrat
Hamzah —
rakam
album tidak
tercapai

AUSTRALIA

Tasmania

Color the Australian flag.

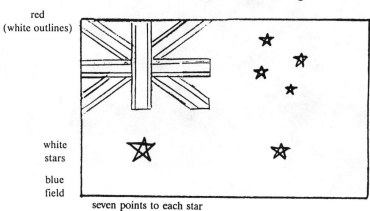

Can you name these places?

1. _____ .
2. _____ .
3. _____ .

Answers: Perth, Sydney, Melbourne

45

AUSTRALIA

Australia lies southeast of Asia. It is the world's largest island and the smallest continent. It is bounded by the Indian Ocean on the west and the Pacific Ocean on the east. The closest neighbors to Australia are New Zealand and Southeast Asia. The name Australia means *Southland* but many call Australia the *land down under.* Australia consists of six states: New South Wales, Queensland, Victoria, Tasmania, South Australia and Western Australia.

Australia is a member of the British Commonwealth of Nations. The Union Jack in the Australian flag represents Australia's membership in the Commonwealth. The six seven-pointed stars in the flag represent the six Australian states. The southern cross, like the flag, is also an Australian national symbol.

Many Australians are descended from British ancestors. The language spoken in Australia is English, but Australian speech has its own distinct character. (See VOCABULARY.) Life in Australia is a lot like that in the United States: for instance, you'd find plenty of traffic jams, buses, trains, stores and shopping centers there.

Australian holidays are similar to those celebrated by many Americans. There are some differences, though. For example, in Australia Easter Monday is a holiday as well as Easter Sunday. The day after Christmas is also a holiday. Instead of a sleigh, Father Christmas comes by plane. Since December 25 is one of the hottest days in Australia, Australians can celebrate Christmas at the beach! (Australia's warmest weather comes in the winter months and the coldest weather in the summer because Australia is located south of the equator.)

In Australia, children must attend school until they are fifteen. School starts in February instead of September and closes before Christmas.

Many unusual animals live in Australia, such as the Koala and the Platypus. Australia's Coat of Arms contains two other native Australian animals: the Emu and the Kangaroo (see below).

Koala from Australia

AUSTRALIAN ACTIVITIES

Children of Australia enjoy playing cricket, pin the tail on the kangaroo, and hopscotch. They also enjoy singing these popular songs.

Waltzing Matilda

Waltzing Matilda is a story of a hike taken by a tramp carrying a swag (blanket roll). The tramp steals a sheep beside a stream and shoves it in a food bag (tucker bag). The squatter (landowner) who owns the sheep and three soldiers come after the tramp, who jumps into the stream and drowns.

First Verse

> *Once a jolly swagman camped by a billa-*
> *bong*
> *Under the shade of a coolibah tree*
> *And he sang as he watched and waited*
> *by the billabong*
> *You'll come a waltzing Matilda with me.*

Chorus

> *Waltzing Matilda, Waltzing Matilda,*
> *You'll come a waltzing Matilda with me,*
> *And he sang as he watched and waited*
> *while the kettle boiled*
> *You'll come a waltzing Matilda with me.*

Second Verse

> *Down came a jumbuck to drink at that*
> *billabong*
> *Up jumped the swagman and grabbed*
> *him with glee,*
> *And he shoved that jumbuck into his*
> *tuckerbag,*
> *You'll come a waltzing Matilda with me.*

Repeat Chorus

Kookaburra

> *Koo-ka-bur-ra sits on an old gum tree,*
> *Merry, merry king of the bush is he,*
> *Laugh, koo-ka-bur-ra, laugh, koo-ka-bur-ra,*
> *Gay your life must be.*

Australian girl painting   Photo by Alma David

RECILPES

Australian Meat Pie

1 pound ground beef
½ C. ketchup
½ C. chopped onion
dash of salt
1 8" pie shell
1 T. Worchestershire sauce
½ C. evaporated milk
⅓ C. bread crumbs
½ t. oregano
dash pepper
1 C. shredded cheddar cheese

Combine beef, milk, ketchup, bread crumbs, onion and dry seasonings. Put in pie shell and bake at 350 degrees about 35 minutes. Mix Worchestershire sauce and cheese and spread on top of pie. Bake at 350 degrees until cheese melts.

Pumpkin Soup
fresh pumpkin
onion
butter
milk
allspice

Cube the inside of a fresh pumpkin. Cut the top off the pumpkin and keep it for a replaceable lid. Scoop the insides of the pumpkin so you can use the shell as a serving bowl. Saute 1 cup (or more, if desired) onions in butter. Add the pumpkin, allspice and 1 cup of milk. Put into a blender and blend until a thick soup consistency. Add more milk, if necessary. Serve in your pumpkin shell for an added touch!

VOCABULARY

dinkum Aussie—100% Australian
dinky dye—everything is going well
rubbers—rainboots
bumpers—barretts
lift—elevator
fairy floss—cotton candy
bash—party
poor cow—someone you feel sorry for
Waltzing Matilda—hike

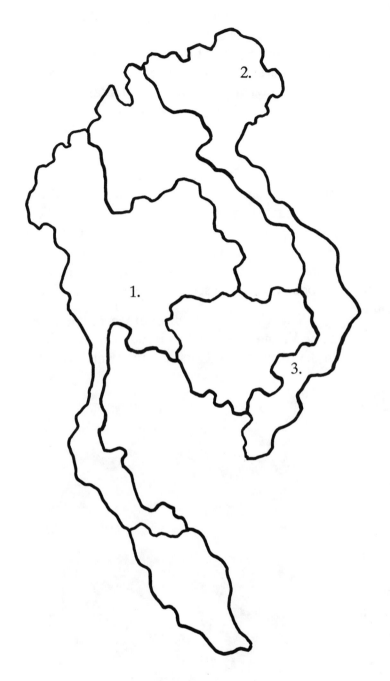

VIETNAM

Can you name these places?

1. _____.
2. _____.
3. _____.

Color the Vietnamese flag.

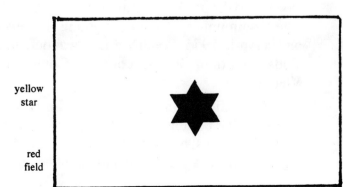

yellow
star

red
field

VIETNAM

Vietnam is a country in southeast Asia, south of China. It is about as large as California, but has over twice as many people California does. It is a long country shaped like the letter "s." Hanoi, the capital, is Vietnam's second largest city with a population of over 1.5 million people. Ho Chi Minh City, known as Saigon before the Vietnam war, is the largest city, with a population of over 3.5 million people. Haiphong is another important Vietnamese city. It is the manufacturing center and main seaport in that portion of the country formerly known as North Vietnam. The weather in Vietnam is tropical. Monsoons and dry seasons alternate.

For much of its history, Vietnam has been the subject of disputes and wars among other countries trying to gain or maintain control of the small country. At various times, the Japanese, French, Chinese and Vietminh-Communists waged war on Vietnam soil trying to establish control.

In May, 1954, at the Geneva Conference, a decision was made to divide Vietnam temporarily into two zones. The northern zone, called North Vietnam, was to be controlled by the Communists and the southern zone, called South Vietnam, was to be controlled by the non-communist Vietnamese. In 1956, however, the Communists decided they wanted complete control of the country. This move by the Communists set off the Vietnam War. Communist countries, such as China and Russia, sent aid to North Vietnam, while non-communist countries, such as the United States, sent aid to South Vietnam. The United States sent thousands of troops and millions of dollars of aid to South Vietman. In 1973, the United States withdrew the last of its troops and the participants agreed to a cease-fire. The Communists continued fighting, however, and in April, 1975, South Vietnam was defeated. Today Vietnam is one country, Communist Vietnam.

The official language of Vietnam is Vietnamese. The population of Vietnam is made up of Vietnamese, Chinese, Cambodians and Montagnards. Montagnards are dark-skinned people of mixed ethnic background. Most Vietnamese live on the river deltas and coastal plains. The Chinese live in the cities and the Cambodians in the rural areas. Many Cambodians are farmers. The Montagnards live in the mountains.

Many Vietnamese are physically small people. They have straight black hair, high cheekbones, and wide faces. Many of the Vietnamese people wear cotton jackets, trousers, and sandals. Most of the people use bicycles for transportation. They eat fish, rice, and vegetables. The Vietnamese have a great respect for learning and most of the Vietnamese people can read and write. Vietnam has elementary, middle, and high schools, vocational schools, and colleges.

The Communists discourage religion, but some Vietnamese practice Buddhism and believe in the teachings of Confucianism and Taoism.

50

SONG OF THE VIETNAMESE CHILDREN

The children sing this song in a circle, holding hands and skipping. They change directions after each line.

Cun nhau mua chung quant la cung nhau mua vong quanh.
Cun nhau mua chung quant la ta cung nhau mua deu.
Nam tay nhau, bat tay nhau ta cung vui mua vui.
Nam tay nhau, bat tay nhau ta cung nhau mu a diw.

ACTIVITY:
Draw some Vietnamese people based on the information given on the previous page.

MID-AUTUMN FESTIVAL "TET TRUNG—THU"

The children in Vietnam celebrate the mid-autumn festival, a celebration of the full moon of the fifteenth day of the eight month of the lunar year. The full moon brings joy to the people. During the night, the children sing and dance. They drink tea and eat cakes shaped like the round face of the moon. These cakes are called moon cakes or mid-autumn cakes. They carry lanterns, which they often make themselves. There are often contests to see who made the best lantern. After the celebration, the children gather around their parents or grandparents to watch the full moon and listen to stories of Vietnam.

RECITES

The Vietnamese people eat a lot of rice and vegetables with small pieces of shrimp, beef or other meats.

Rice Vietnamese style is made by adding onion, garlic, ketchup, soy sauce, carrots, and eggs to the rice.

Spring Rolls

Rice paper
Cabbage
Small pieces of meat (pork, shrimp, etc.)
Onion and/or other finely chopped vegetables

Soak rice paper until it is soft. Combine other ingredients. Put mixture in rice paper, fold and deep fry until lightly browned. Serve with soy sauce or a sauce of vinegar and carrot slivers.

Sweet Soup

5 C. water
1½ C. sugar
1 can green beans
⅓ C. coconut

Combine ingredients and bring to a boil. Serve hot.

VOCABULARY

one—*một*
two—*hai*
three—*ba*
four—*bốn*
five—*năm*
six—*saú*
seven—*bâỹ*
eight—*tám*
nine—*chiń*
ten—*mửỏi*

52

THE CARIBBEAN & LATIN AMERICA

West Indies

Mexico

Central America

Panama

South America

Brazil

Carrying rocks on a burro's back.

BAHAMAS

Can you name these places?

1. _____.

2. _____.

3. _____.

Answers: Freeport, Nassau, Great Inagua Island

Color the Bahamian flag.

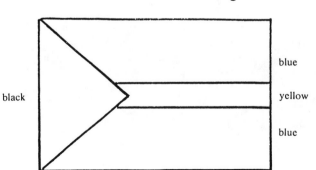

black

blue

yellow

blue

55

THE BAHAMAS

Columbus, sailing for Spain, first sighted San Salvador, an island in the Bahamas, in 1492. The original natives of the Bahamian islands were the Arawak Indians and the warlike, cannibalistic Caribs. The Spanish were not interested in colonizing the Bahamas but they enslaved these *Lucayans*, island people, and took them to Hispaniola.

The Bahamas then remained uninhabited for almost a century until the English arrived. The British decided to colonize the Bahamas and by the late eighteenth century, British control of the islands was well established. The British colonists built many houses and churches, particularly on Nassau, the most populated of the islands. The colonists established large plantations on the islands for cultivating crops, and introduced slavery to the islands. Since slave ships coming from West Africa stopped here before going on to Cuba, the Bahamian planters had first choice among the slaves for sale. The planters thus picked out and bought the more civilized and desirable slaves. The slave trade was abolished by the British in 1807 but it continued in North America and Europe. In 1834, slavery was abolished in the Bahamas. Today a large part of the Bahamian population is made up of blacks who are descendents of West African slaves.

Today the Bahamian economy is largely dependent on real estate investment and Bahama's booming tourist trade. The currency in the Bahamas is the Bahamian dollar which is comparable to the U.S. dollar in value, although it fluctuates slightly. English is the language spoken by the Bahamians.

The Bahamas are very popular with tourists. The Straw Market, casinos and conch are favorite experiences for the tourist in Nassau. Freeport offers the visitor an international bazaar and a large shopping center in addition to the Straw Market. Perfume, batik, and straw handbags, dolls, hats and mats are some of the island's best bargains. Conch, the lovely pink and white sea shell, is made into beautiful earrings, pins and other jewelry. You can eat the meat of the conch in such dishes as conch fritters, conch chowder, cracked conch and conch salad.

Despite the benefits enjoyed by the Bahamas due to the tourist trade, many of the people of the Bahamas remain uneducated. Families in the Bahamas are very large. The schools in general are very poor and overcrowded. One of the major concerns of the Bahamian government today is improving the Bahamas' school system.

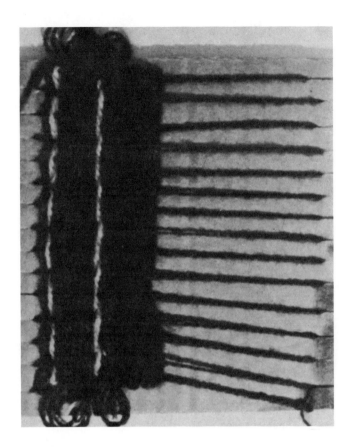

ART PROJECTS FROM THE BAHAMAS

You can accomplish simple weaving with just a piece of cardboard. Cut a series of small parallel slits along each of opposite edges of the cardboard, as shown. Wrap yarn around and around the cardboard, anchored in the slits. Weave another piece of yarn over and under the first yarn until the piece is finished. Cut the back pieces of yarn and tie them off to create your finished product.

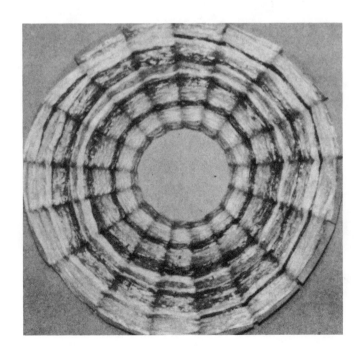

Bahamian design woven with colored straw.

RECIPES

A favorite dish in the Bahamas is Conch. It is the meat inside the familiar pretty pink shell that we put to our ear to hear the ocean. Although conch may be hard to find outside the Bahamas and Florida, we've included these recipes with the hope that your fish market can get you some. Conch is tough and must be pounded the way abalone is tenderized on the Pacific Coast. Bahamian food is spicy, so use plenty of seasoning to give the conch the authentic taste of Bahamian cooking.

Conch is not an endangered species. A mature female conch, one six years or older, will lay 300,000 to 500,000 eggs three times a year. A conch does not lose its shell, but grows up with it to an average size of 1½ to 2 pounds. Conch can be eaten raw or with a dash of lime juice, or cooked in conch chowder, cracked conch, or conch fritters.

Conch Fritters

2 medium conchs finely diced
2 C. flour
2 t. baking powder
salt
1 C. water
1 stalk celery, chopped
1 onion, chopped
½ green pepper, chopped
1 T. tomato paste
dash of paprika
dash of thyme

Combine flour, salt and baking powder. Separately, combine celery, onions, pepper and conch in mixing bowl. Add water and flour alternately, beating batter thoroughly after each addition. Add thyme, tomato paste and paprika. Beat well and drop into deep fat and fry until brown.

Cracked Conch (pronounced "konk")

1½ pounds conch, tenderized
¾ C. fine bread crumbs
2 large beaten eggs
6 T. lime juice
dash of allspice, garlic powder, hot pepper sauce

Mix allspice, garlic powder and bread crumbs in shallow bowl. Dip conch into beaten eggs then roll in bread crumb mixture. Fry until brown. Turn and fry other side. Pour lime juice and hot pepper sauce on just before serving.

HAITI

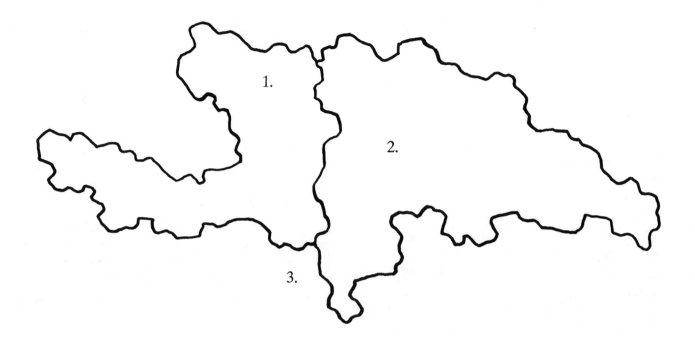

1.

2.

3.

Can you name these places?

1. _____.
2. _____.
3. _____.

Color the Haitian flag.

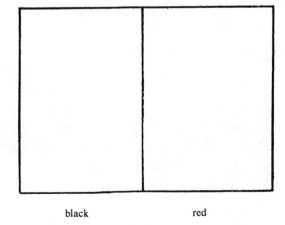

black   red

HAITI

Christopher Columbus discovered Haiti in 1492. The Spanish returned to this "paradise" the following year and were welcomed by the native Arawak Indians. In return the Spanish enslaved both the Arawaks and the cannibalistic Carib Indians, also native to Haiti, and forced the Indians to work in Spanish mines and plantations. The Indians soon died out and the Spaniards began to engage in the West African slave trade to replace the Indian workers.

The French took control of Haiti in 1697, renaming the island Saint Dominique, and it became the richest colony in the New World. Despite Haiti's prosperity, however, the slaves on Haiti were badly treated. In the late eighteenth century, led by Toussaint L'Ouverture (known as the "George Washington of Haiti"), the slaves successfully rebelled against the oppressive Haitian aristocracy. When Napoleon came to power, he sent French troops to regain control of the Haitian colony. The Haitians defeated the troops and in 1804 Haiti gained its freedom from foreign control or rule.

Out of fear that the French would return, a man named Henri Chistophe organized the building of the Citadelle La Ferriere in 1808. The Citadelle was a fortress designed to help the Haitians defend themselves against French invasion. The French never returned, however, and the fort was never used.

Without the French, the mines and lands of Haiti fell into disuse. The world seemed to forget Haiti. Since the people there were uneducated, disease, poverty and superstition became prevalent.

In 1917, the United States entered World War I. Since Haiti guarded the eastern entrance to the Panama Canal, Americans moved into Haiti, bringing aid and constructing needed buildings. Twenty years later, however, the Americans left, and the island was again on its own.

Today the Haitian tourist trade is growing in towns such as Port au Prince, the capital, and Cap Hatien. Tourists are very important to the Haitians. Most Haitians are very poor. Whatever goods a family can sell to tourists mean precious extra income, even though the prices of the goods may seem very low to an American tourist. Many Haitian families help support themselves by selling such items as beads made from coffee beans, carved mahogany bowls and figures, brightly painted pictures, hand embroidered blouses, and woven baskets and hats.

Many Haitians live in mud huts and experience a life of poverty and disease. Since most of these people can afford only one meal a day, they eat early to give themselves the energy to get through the day. They consume the breadfruit, avocados, bananas and coffee which they grow themselves.

Voodoo is very popular with most Haitians, although the official faith of Haiti is Roman Catholicism. The people of Haiti speak Creole, a French dialect unique to Haiti. French is the official language and most literature you find there is printed in French.

HAITIAN ART

Haitian art is a multi-faceted form of art which has been in existence for hundreds of years. It has not always been understood or appreciated, however, by the rest of the world. It represents a link between the world of voodoo and the Catholic religion, and a link between a primitive world and modern life. This is a sample of a Haitian picture. The colors are bright red, blue, yellow, green, white and pink.

This is a pen and ink picture of a Haitian woman carrying a basket of fruit on her head. This is a common practice among Haitian women.

This is an elementary school in Haiti. The children dress in uniforms. The little girls were very camera-shy.

VOODOO DOLL

Voodoo is very popular among most Haitians. Voodoo is a blend of African and traditional Christian beliefs. Believers worship gods they believe control the rain, water, love, war and all other aspects of life. The religion involves many rituals, ceremonies and dances. Often believers try to become possessed by gods during these ceremonies. The *ungan* is the high priest who performs the ceremonies. The *dembala* is the snake dance, the *aidae* is the water dance (like a baptism), and the *petro* is a fire dance, where participants walk on coals and eat fire.

RECIPES

Plat National*

1 C. dried kidney beans or 1 10 oz. can, drained
3 C. water
2-4 strips bacon
1-2 medium onions
1 C. cooked rice
dash of cloves, salt, pepper
few drops of hot pepper sauce

Soak dried beans overnight in 3 cups water, then simmer, covered, over low heat until they are tender (about one hour). If canned beans are used, heat until warm and omit the 3 cups of water. Fry bacon, then saute onions in the grease. Add all the ingredients to the beans: crumbled bacon, onions, cloves, salt, pepper and hot pepper sauce (as desired). Serve over cooked rice.

Melongene**

1 eggplant, chopped
1 clove garlic, minced
1 tomato, chopped
2 T. oil
1 onion, chopped
1 green pepper, chopped
salt, pepper to taste

Sautee onion, pepper, garlic in oil. Add tomato and eggplant, salt and pepper and cook for ten minutes.

VOCABULARY

These Arawak words are used in our vocabulary.

> *avocado*
> *barbecue*
> *buccaneer*
> *canoe*
> *cannibal*
> *cay*
> *guava*
> *hammock*
> *hurricane*
> *iguana*
> *maize*
> *potato*
> *tobacco*

Women carrying straw baskets in Haiti.

63

JAMAICA

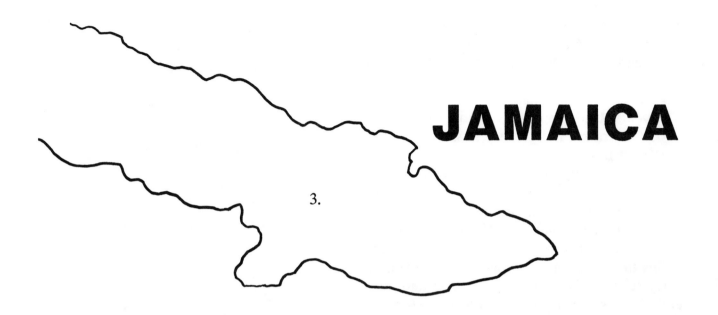

3.

1.

2.

Color the Jamaican flag.

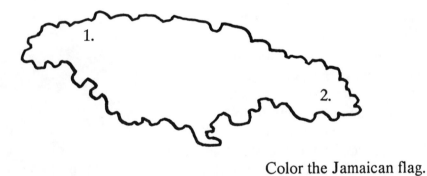

green

yellow

black

black

green

Can you name these places?

1. _____ .

2. _____ .

3. _____ .

JAMAICA

The island of Jamaica is an independent country located in the Caribbean Sea, approximately ninety miles south of Cuba. It is strategically important since its location controls the entrance to the Caribbean Sea. A United States naval and air base is located near Kingston.

The island was discovered by Columbus in 1494, and ruled by Spain for over one hundred fifty years. Under Spanish rule, approximately 100,000 Arawak Indians died in slavery; a few hundred survived.

When the British seized Jamaica in 1655, a group of Indians and Africans, former Spanish slaves, fled into Jamaica's mountain areas. These "exiles" became known as "Maroons," and a mystique developed about them because of their ability to avoid capture or control by the British. They successfully evaded British rule until the early 1700's. During Spanish rule, few Africans had been imported into Jamaica as slaves. During the eighteenth century, under British rule, however, many Africans were imported. At one point as many as 300,000 African slaves were at work on the plantations that made Jamaica the leading sugar producer in the world. Slavery was abolished there in 1838.

English is the official language of Jamaica. In 1962, Jamaica became an independent member of the British Commonwealth of Nations. The political system of Jamaica reflects the influence of the British parliamentary form of government. In Jamaica, there are two major political parties: The People's National Party and The Jamaica Labor Party. In 1980, The People's National Party, a socialist party in favor of government ownership of businesses, was defeated in the national election. The Jamaica Labor Party, a socialist party which is generally pro-business and in favor of free enterprise, was elected to power.

Tourism is an important industry in Jamaica. Ocho Rios, a port town sixty miles east of Montego Bay, is a popular area. Beautiful hotels line the tranquil north coast. Dunn's River Falls, 690 feet high, opens into the sea. A natural stairway there can be climbed with the aid of a guide. Working plantations are also located near Ocho Rios.

Jamaica is known for its straw goods, wooden statues and beautiful batiks. These popular items are sold in the straw markets.

Rafting down the Rio Grande River is a very popular sport. Local women still wash their clothes in the river and lay them on the rocks to dry as has been done for generations.

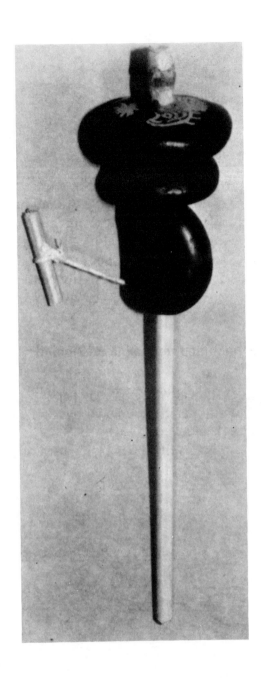

THE JAMAICAN YO-YO

This yo-yo is one of the most popular toys in Jamaica. It is based on the same principle as the popular American yo-yo. The Jamaican yo-yo is made with three shiny bean pods called *cacoons*. To use it, a child pulls the string outward and then releases it, which causes the string to rewind on its own.

Practice playing with the yo-yo and have contests with your friends to see who has practiced the most.

RECIPES

Baked Bananas

6 bananas
1 orange, cut into chunks-peeled
2 T. frozen orange juice
2 T. lemon juice
⅓ C. sugar
dash of cinnamon and/or nutmeg

Preheat oven to 325 degrees. Combine all ingredients but bananas. Place peeled bananas in baking dish and pour mixture over them. Bake 20-30 minutes and serve.

Fish Stew

fresh fish (remove head and tail)
3 qt. water
1 T. butter
dash salt, pepper, garlic
1 small onion, chopped
⅓ C. chopped green peppers
1 16 oz. can tomatoes
1 cube chicken bouillon
leftover vegetables

Cook the fish in 3 qts. of boiling water. Add salt, pepper, garlic. Saute onion and green pepper in butter and add to soup. Add a can of tomatoes and leftover vegetables (potatoes, carrots, etc.) Add 1 cube of chicken bouillon and continue to cook for about 45 minutes.

Ham Banana Rolls*

4 slices boiled ham
mustard
4 firm bananas
3 t. melted butter

Cheese Sauce:
cheddar cheese soup OR mixture of melted cheese, milk and small quantity of flour

Preheat oven to 350 degrees. Spread ham with mustard. Peel bananas and wrap in a ham slice. Brush with melted butter. Place in greased baking dish and cover with Cheese Sauce. Bake 30 minutes or until bananas are easily pierced with a fork.

Other popular Jamaican foods include:

Curried goat
Jerk pork—meat which has had peppers pounded into it and has been cooked over an open pit
Red beans and rice
Pattys—pastries filled with spicy meat mixtures

PANAMA

Color the Panamanian flag.

white
field

blue
star

red

red
star

blue

white
field

Can you name these places?

1. _____ .
2. _____ .
3. _____ .

PANAMA

Panama is most famous for the Panama Canal, which allows ships to take a "short-cut" from the Atlantic to the Pacific Ocean instead of having to travel all the way around the southern tip of South America. The French began to build a canal in 1882 but abandoned the effort seven years later.

In 1903, led by President Theodore Roosevelt, the United States began work on the canal. George Washington Goethals supervised construction. On May 20, 1913, the Panama Canal was completed. It was an enormously expensive project and the engineering feat of its time. Twenty-five thousand people died during the construction, most from malaria.

The locks of the canal are enormous—110 feet wide and 1000 feet long. They are taller than the Eiffel Tower. It usually takes about eight hours to travel through the Panama Canal, although larger ships may take a little longer. The first two and one-fourth hours are spent going through the canal's concrete locks and the next five and three-fourths hours traveling through the beautiful Panamanian jungle.

After the ship is in the first lock, the huge gates close and water pours into the lock at the rate of 3,000,000 gallons per minute. This water raises the ship to the level of Gatun Lake, eighty-five feet above sea level. The ship then cruises across the lake to the Gatun Locks, in which the process is reversed and the ship is lowered back to sea level. It can then head out into the ocean.

The price charged for passage through the canal is high, but lower than the cost of travelling around the tip of South America. The highest price ever paid to pass through the Canal was $89,154.62, which was paid by the ship the Queen Elizabeth II. The lowest price ever paid was $.36, paid in 1936 by Richard Halliburton, a swimmer.

As a result of a treaty which was signed by President Jimmy Carter and ratified by the United States Senate in 1978, control of the Panama Canal will be returned to Panama by the year 2000.

The girl is wearing a *pollera,* an embroidered blouse and skirt of white cotton. Panamanians adapted and changed this type of Spanish dress to suit their climate and lifestyle.

Festival Figures, UNICEF.

PANAMA'S FESTIVALS

Many festivals are held each year in Panama. Many towns in Panama have a patron saint, and they often hold a festival on their saint's day. In addition, many festivals are held during *Carnival*. The *Carnival* celebration takes place just before Lent. (The forty weekdays between Ash Wednesday and Easter, known as Lent, are observed by Roman Catholics, Eastern and some Protestant churches as a time for penitence and fasting.) The *Carnival* lasts for four days. There are street dances, costumes, parades, and music. Folk art, such as the *mola*, is displayed. The *mola* is a type of art, made famous by the San Blas Indians, where designs are cut out of cloth and these stencils are placed on top of each other to create a finished piece.

The monetary unit of Panama is the *balboa*. It has the same value as the U.S. dollar and is used interchangably. Find out what the monetary units of the other countries studied are and make a chart:

COUNTRY	MONEY NAME	SUBDIVISION
Panama	balboa	100 centesimos
Russia	ruble	100 kopecks
India	rupee	100 paise
Japan	yen	100 sen
Haiti	gourde	100 centimes
Mexico	peso	100 centavos
France	franc	100 centimes

RECIPES

Guacamole

2 large avocados—peeled and chopped
1 tomato, peeled
½ onion, chopped
2 cloves garlic, chopped
2 T. wine vinegar
½ t. salt

Place all ingredients in an electric blender. Blend 60 to 90 seconds. Serve with corn chips or on a salad.

*Picadillo**

2 T. oil
2 garlic cloves
1 large chopped onion
1 pound ground beef
2 ripe tomatoes, chopped (or canned tomatoes)
½ C. raisins
⅓ C. pimento stuffed olives
1 green pepper

Saute onion and garlic in oil. Add meat, seasonings and wine. Add other ingredients and cook until heated. Serve over white rice.

National Coat of Arms

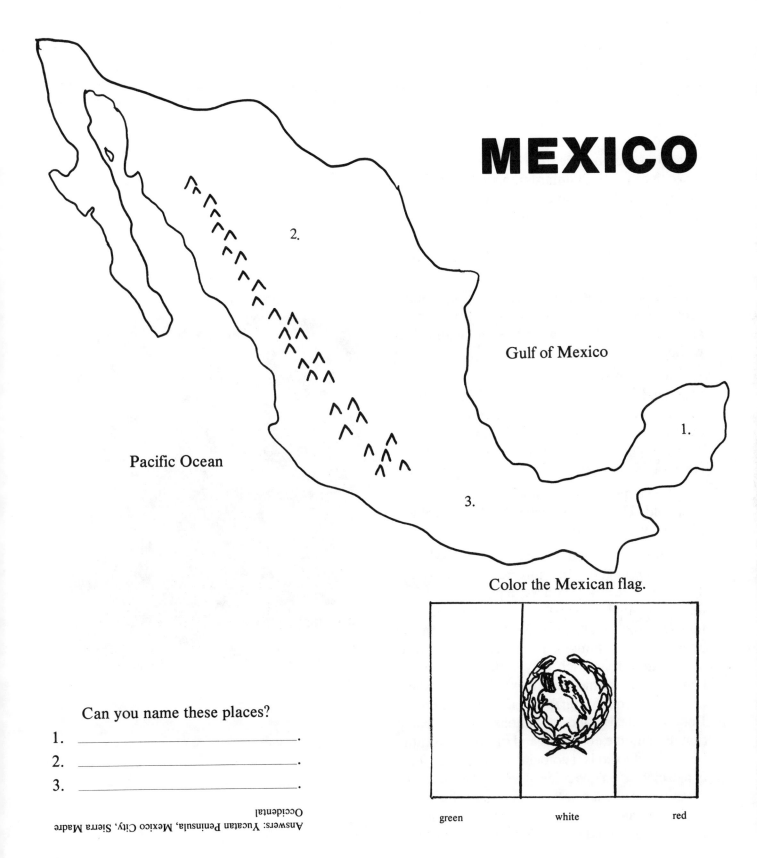

MEXICO

Gulf of Mexico

2.

Pacific Ocean

1.

3.

Color the Mexican flag.

Can you name these places?

1. _____.

2. _____.

3. _____.

green   white   red

MEXICO

Mexico is a large country located directly south of the United States. Its terrain includes mountains covered with snow, deserts, and flatlands. It is bounded by water on two sides - the Pacific Ocean to the west and the Gulf of Mexico to the east. The capital is Mexico City.

The people from Mexico are called Mexicans. Years ago, many Indian tribes lived in Mexico. Later, people from Spain came to Mexico to live. These Spaniards married the Indians. Today most of the people of Mexico are *mestizo*— half Indian and half Spanish. Mexicans speak Spanish.

The Mexicans are a very religious people. Most of them are Roman Catholic. The Mexicans have many festivals or *fiestas*. They usually celebrate saints' days. At fiestas, Mexicans eat and drink heartily. Most fiestas end with a fireworks display.

Mexican food is very popular now in our country. Mexicans eat chicken, meats and many fresh fruits and vegetables. The main meal of the day in Mexico is lunch. Each day, the family comes together at home to enjoy a big feast. Afterwards, they often enjoy a nap called a *siesta*.

The children start school when they are six years old. They attend high school, then college or a vocational school.

Mexicans play many sports: basketball, soccer, swimming, bullfighting and cockfighting. There are also many wonderful places and things to see in Mexico. The Indians of long ago left temples, pyramids, and many colorful mural paintings. The famous Diego Rivera's murals are located in Mexico City's National Palace. Children love the historic Chapultepec Park where many of them have birthday parties. The Ballet Folklorico de Mexico is a famous Mexican ballet that uses native costumes and dances. It is quite beautiful. Taxco is a colonial silver center. This quaint city has unique colonial houses and churches, silver workshops, a native market, and hundreds of shops selling silver and gold jewelry and colonial crafts. Acapulco is famous for its beautiful beaches and cliff divers. These divers thrill viewers as they dive between cliffs into the sea from incredible heights. Teotihuacan, the archaeological zone of Mexico, contains the pyramids of the Sun and the Moon. It is breathtaking to climb atop these pyramids and think back to the time of their construction.

LA PINATA (pronounced pin-ya-tuh)

On Christmas Eve, the children of Mexico help celebrate the occasion with a *pinata*. A *pinata* is usually made in the shape of an animal, bird or person. It is often made of paper mache and covered with colored crepe paper or tissue paper. It may also be made of clay or it can be a paper bag made to look like an animal. It is hollow and is filled with candies and small gifts. It is hung from the ceiling so it swings freely. One at a time, the children are blindfolded and each takes a turn to swing at the pinata with a stick. When it breaks, all the children rush to pick up the treats.

SOMBRERO AND SERAPE

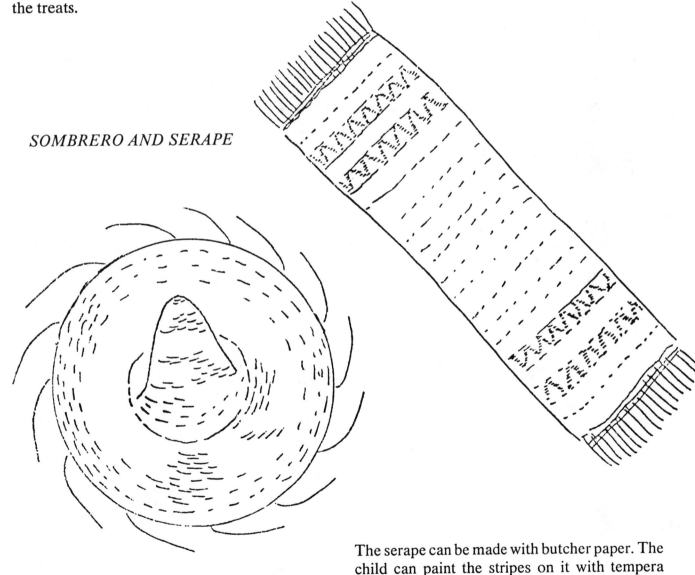

The serape can be made with butcher paper. The child can paint the stripes on it with tempera paint.

75

Directions for dancing the Mexican Hat Dance
LA RASPA

Partners face each other, left shoulder to left shoulder. Beginning right, step from heel to toe 8 times. Turn to face opposite direction (right shoulder to right shoulder) and repeat. Repeat action, facing opposite direction (left shoulder to left shoulder). Repeat the action. Hook right elbows, left hands held high. Take 8 running steps, clapping on the eighth step. Repeat action.

The movements are the same for boy and girl. To begin, the girl holds her skirt and the boy holds clasped hands behind his back.

SPANISH FIESTA RECIPES

Tacos

Cooked ground beef
Shredded onion
Shredded cheese
Shredded lettuce
Shredded tomato
Taco Shells
taco seasoning (packets available at grocery store, follow directions to prepare with beef)
Taco sauce (many brands available at grocery store)

Prepare cooked ground beef with taco seasoning. Spoon this mixture into taco shell and top with onion and cheese. Place in oven until cheese is melted. Top with lettuce and chopped tomatoes and taco sauce.

(Instructions for tacos are given on taco shells packages.)

Enchiladas

Cooked ground beef
Shredded onion
Shredded cheese
Enchilada sauce
Canned or frozen tortillas

Dip tortillas into enchilada sauce. Place flat on slightly greased cookie sheet. Drop ground beef, onion and cheese onto the enchilada-sauce-covered tortilla. Repeat until the stack has as many enchiladas as you wish. Place in 300 degree oven until heated thoroughly--about 30 minutes.

Refried Beans - Frijoles (pronounced free-ho-lays)

Heat a can of refried beans and top with grated cheese.

Spanish Rice

Add a spoonful of taco sauce to the top of cooked white rice.

Straw donkey carrying clay pitchers for water.

Nachos

Round tortilla chips
Taco Sauce
Shredded cheddar cheese
Green chilies

Put small amount of sauce, cheese and chilies on top of chips and bake at 350 degrees for 5 minutes.

VOCABULARY

one—*uno*
two—*dos*
three—*tres*
four—*quatro*
five—*cinco*
six—*seis*
seven—*siete*
eight—*ocho*
nine—*nueve*
ten—*diez*

Good day—*Buenos dias.*
Good afternoon—*Buenas tardes.*
Good night—*Buenos noches.*

Thank you—*Gracias.*
Please—*Por favor.*

What is your name?
¿ Como se llamo usted?

BRAZIL

1.

2.

3.

Color the Brazilian flag.

green
field

blue
circle

white
stars

yellow
diamond

Can you name these places?

1. _____.

2. _____.

3. _____.

Answers: Amazon River, Brasília, Atlantic Ocean

79

BRAZIL

Brazil is the largest country in South America and ranks fifth in size in the world. It occupies the eastern half of South America and has a 4,500 mile coastline on the Atlantic Ocean.

A Portuguese navigator, Pedro Cabral, discovered Brazil in 1500. At that time Brazil was occupied by several Indian tribes. During the next few hundred years, colonists from Portugal moved into the interior and built large sugar plantations. They brought with them many African slaves to work the plantations. Slavery was abolished in Brazil in 1888.

In 1808, the king of Portugal, Don Joao VI, was defeated by the French Emperor, Napoleon Bonaparte. He left Portugal and instituted a government in exile in Brazil, establishing a kingdom in that country. In 1822, after Don Joao returned to Portugal, his son Pedro proclaimed Brazil's independence and became Brazil's Emperor. In 1889, a republic was established: the United States of Brazil. In 1930, Getulio Vargas seized control of the government with the aid of the military and ruled Brazil as a dictator. Brazil established a democratic government in 1956 which lasted until 1964. In 1956 the capital was moved from Rio de Janerio to Brasilia. In 1967, the country was officially named the Federative Republic of Brazil.

Brazil is known for its major river system. The Amazon River, which flows through Brazil, is the world's largest river. It has an enormous flow and forces fresh water as far as one hundred miles into the Atlantic. The rivers in Brazil provide a valuable means of transportation.

A majority of the people in Brazil are Portuguese, Africans and mulattoes. Today most of the few remaining Indians live deep in the forests along the banks of the Amazon River. In addition, there are Italians, Germans, Japanese, Jews and Arabs living in Brazil. The language is Portuguese. A majority of the population is Roman Catholic.

Brazil has a compulsory free education system at the primary level which consists of programs which range from three to five years: five years in large cities, four years in the towns and three years in many villages and remote areas. Middle schools, the equivalent of junior and senior high schools in the United States, are available to students aged 12 to 18 who pass an entrance exam.

The rainforests in Brazil have become a major worldwide environmental issue. The farmers near and in the Amazon burn the trees, and the gases released from this are harming the earth's ozone layer. This destruction of the forest is also hurting many plant and animal species, threatening them with extinction. Environmental action groups, worried about the future of our planet, are trying to move the world's governments to protect endangered rainforests.

The Mardi Gras costume is in celebration of the festival celebrated in many Latin Countries.

FUTEBAL
Soccer

Futebal, or soccer, is the national sport of Brazil. Pele, a word famous soccer player, is from Brazil. Futebal is a sport that is played with two teams, each, each with eleven players. The game lasts four quarters. The playing field has a goal at each end. The players start in the center of the field and try to move the ball toward their opponents' goal. They can only use their feet or heads to move the ball - no hands! A team scores points when it gets the ball into the other team's goal (pictured below). Each team has a *goalie* whose job it is to keep the ball OUT of the goal. The team which scores the most points wins.

GOAL

RECIPES

Cocoa*

¼ C. water
3 T. cocoa
2 T. sugar
2 C. milk
1 t. vanilla

Bring water to a boil. Add cocoa and sugar and stir. Turn heat to low, add milk and cook for a minute. Remove from heat, add vanilla and pour into cups.

Cocoa and chocolate come from the beans of the cacao tree, native to Central and South America. Cocoa has been a favorite drink for hundreds of years.

Choclos (Ears of corn)*

Ears of corn grow very large in parts of South America. They are cooked over charcoal or steamed.

ears of corn
butter
salt
water

Remove the husks and silk from the corn. Boil the corn in water about five minutes or until it is tender. Serve with butter and salt.

Guava

Guava is a red or yellow fruit about the size of a tangerine. It is popular in Brazil, Hawaii, Cuba and many other warm countries.

Bread
Guava jelly
Spread the bread with the guava and enjoy!

VOCABULARY (Portuguese)

hug—*abraco*
love—*amor*
friend—*amigo (ga)*
classmate—*condiscipula (la)*
idea—*conceito*
wonderful—*marvilhoso*
dawn—*matina*
painting (picture)—*pintura*
sun—*sol*
grapefruit—*toronja*

Guava plant

AFRICA, THE NEAR & MIDDLE EAST

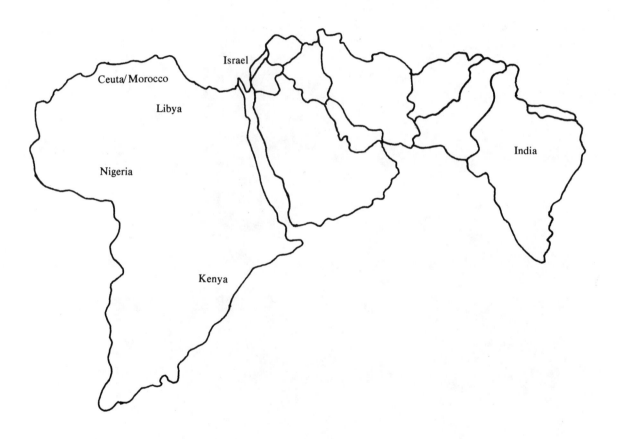

Egyptian children

84

IRAN

Can you name these places?

1. _____ .
2. _____ .
3. _____ .

Color the Iranian flag.

green
stripe

white
stripe

red
stripe

red
emblem

IRAN

Iran is a small country in Southwestern Asia that is bordered by the Soviet Union, Afghanistan, Pakistan, the Gulf of Oman and the Persian Gulf, Iraq, and Turkey.

Iran, once a part of the great Persian empire, is one of the world's oldest countries. The name "Iran" means "Land of the Aryans," a reference to the Aryan people called the Persians who united the country and founded the Persian empire more than 2500 years ago. The Persian empire was ruled by famous leaders such as Cyrus the Great, Darius the Great, and Alexander the Great.

Iran was ruled by a "Shah," which means king, from 1925 until 1979. In the early 1900's oil was discovered in Iran, which gave the country a great deal of wealth. The Shah used this money to modernize the country and improve living and working conditions for the Iranians. In 1979 a revolution broke out and Ayatollah Khomeini, a religious leader, took control of Iran. Now Iran's government is an Islamic republic, and the country's supreme leader is the "faqih." Khomeini died in 1989.

Most of the people in Iran belong to the Sh'i sect of the Muslim religion, which is one of the oldest religions in the world. It is a requirement that all chief government officials belong to the Muslim religion.

The country of Iran consists mostly of a plateau with mountains scattered across it. Iran also has many regions which are deserts. The capital and largest city is Tehran. About half of the people in Iran live in cities; the other half live in rural areas. A small number of people do not have a place where they live all year round. They are called nomads. In the summers they live in the cool mountain valleys, and in the winters they live in the hot lowland plains.

Most Iranians have a close-knit family unit. The father, or another older male, is the "aga," which means "master." He commands total respect and obedience from the other family members. Where old traditions are still followed, it is usual for sons to remain in the family home even after they are married. Traditional clothes for men are cotton shirts and baggy trousers. Women wear a "chador," which is a long cloth used as a head covering, wrap-around, and sometimes as a veil.

Some of the favorite sports of Iran are skiing, polo, wrestling, and weightlifting. Iran has an Olympic Association which trains and finances local athletes for the Olympic games. Iranians also enjoy playing chess, which originated in Iran and India.

Some famous Iranians include Zarathustra, who founded the Mazdaism religion, and Omar Khayyam, an astronomer and poet who wrote the Rubaiyat.

PERSIAN RUGS

Handwoven Oriental rugs have been made in Iran for many centuries. They are valued for their beauty and fine craftsmanship. Artists design the rugs and then skilled weavers weave them. Often the rugs present a picture or scene, not just a design. Many of the rugs are made of wool, but the most expensive rugs are made from silk. Sometimes metallic threads are used to make the rugs even fancier. Rugs made of silk sell for as much as $200,000 in international auctions.

RECIPES

Persian-Style Cold Yogurt Soup

2 tablespoons golden raisins
1 cucumber
2 cups plain yogurt
3/4 teaspoon salt
1/8 teaspoon freshly ground black pepper
1 cup heavy cream
1 cup ice water
2 tablespoons very finely sliced green of scallions
3 tablespoons coarsely chopped walnuts
1 tablespoon minced fresh dill

Soak the raisins in a cup of hot water for an hour, then drain. Peel and grate the cucumber. Put yogurt, salt, pepper into a bowl; beat until creamy. Slowly add one cup ice water and cream, while beating. Add the other ingredients and mix well. If the soup is not to be eaten immediately it should be refrigerated.

Doogh (Persian-Style Yogurt Drink, Flavored with Mint)

1/2 cup plain yogurt
1 1/2 cups ice-cold water
1/4 teaspoon salt
4 ice cubes
2 sprigs fresh mint

Put the yogurt in a bowl. Slowly add ice water, while beating with a fork or whisk. Season with salt. Add ice cubes and garnish with mint.

VOCABULARY

The official language of Iran is Farsi, which is a mixture of ancient Persian and Arabic. Arabic characters and script are used to write Farsi.

imam—*leader*
caliph—*religious leader*
shah—*king*
dasht—*loose sand and stones which cover the deserts*
kavir—*large salt masses found in the deserts*
qanaat—*underground tunnels used by farmers for irrigation*
zurkhaneh—*"House of strength"—athletic club where weight lifters work out*

87

ARABIC NUMBERS

Today we use numbers known as Arabic numerals. Over the centuries the Arabs have started to use a different style for their numbers:

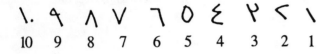

١.	٩	٨	٧	٦	٥	٤	٣	٢	١
10	9	8	7	6	5	4	3	2	1

ACTIVITY

Design your own Persian rug. You can have your rug tell a story, or it can be made up of designs. On a piece of cardboard, glue pieces of colorful construction paper that you have cut out. Cut several pieces of yarn about an inch-long and glue them on two opposite edges of the "rug" to form the fringe.

THE ARABIC ALPHABET

Arabic is read from right to left.

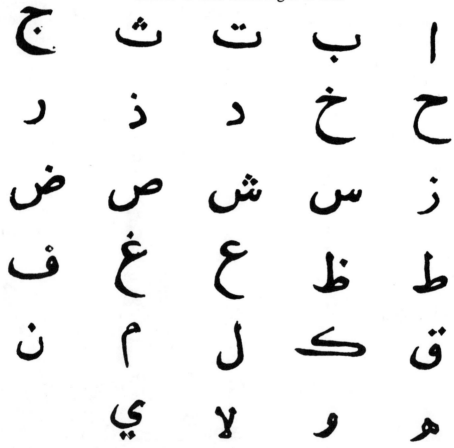

NIGERIA

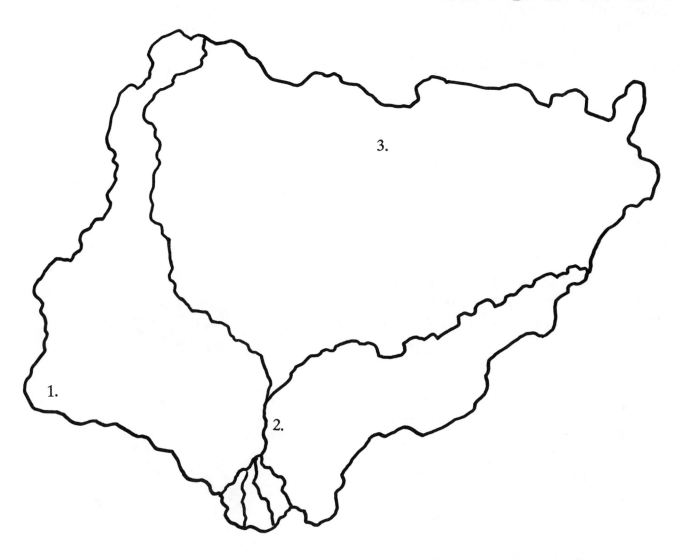

Color the Nigerian flag.

green	white	green

Can you name these places?

1. _____.
2. _____.
3. _____.

Answers: Lagos, Niger River, Kano

89

NIGERIA

Nigeria is a country in West Africa. It is named after the fabulous Niger River, which flows for 2500 miles north, east and south, puzzling and misleading the world until it empties into the Atlantic Ocean through a hundred mouths. The Niger Delta is twice the size of the state of New Jersey. The climate of Nigeria is hot and humid along the sea coast and dry in the north.

Nigeria is Africa's most populous nation. Within its land area of 356,667 square miles lives a population of 107,655,000 people. Lagos (the capital), Kano, and Ibadan are populous cities. The main ethnic groups in the country are the Hausa, Ibo, and Yorubas. The official language is English. There are, however, some 250 ethnic groups represented in Nigeria and over 250 native tongues spoken there. Nigerians are a very religious people. Chritian, Muslim, and Animist are the predominant religions in Nigeria. The Nigerian people also proud, hospitable and sports-minded.

Since independence from Britian in 1960, Nigeria has endured a series of coups and civil wars; however, the country is now achieving civil maturity and economic growth. Hostilities among the Hausa, Ibo and Yorubas no longer exist. The last military regime produced a democratic constitution which it transferred to the civilian government. Several universities have been constructed in Nigeria in recent years to meet some of the country's educational needs.

Nigeria is one of the world's largest producers of petroleum and exporter of crude oil to the United States. Tin, coal, palm oil and peanuts are other products.

The Jos Plateau contains holiday resorts popular both with natives and tourists. When visiting Nigeria, the okra and vegetable soup, the Iba-food of Yorubaland, and the towen shinkafa of Hausaland are too delicious.

The art of Nigeria comes from the city-states of Benin and Ife. Basket weaving there is a necessary skill as well as a beautiful craft. Bronze and copper casting techniques and the weaving of Akwette cloth amaze historians of technology.

The girl is wearing the typical dress of the Yoruba. The head-tie is called a *gele,* the blouse is a *buba,* the wrapper is an *irobirin* and the shawl is an *iborun.* The most popular color in Nigeria is blue. Nigerian boys wear blue *agbadas,* poncho-type shirts with flowing sleeves, over pajama-like trousers.

Festival Figures, UNICEF.

BATIK

Materials: wax, dye, fabric, brush, newspaper, iron

1. Lightly pencil-sketch design on cotton fabric.

2. Apply melted wax to design area. Every area not covered by wax will be dyed.

3. Let wax semi-dry. Run waxed design under cold water.

4. Put the fabric into a dye-bath. Allow fabric to remain until 2 shades darker than desired.

5. Take fabric out of dye and rinse in cold running water until excess dye is removed.

6. Allow fabric to dry

7. Sandwich the dried fabric between newspaper (or newsprint) and press with medium iron to remove wax.

If more than one color is desired, repeat steps 1-6, using the darker dye bath each time. The African batik below has a variety of colors, including yellow, orange, red, and black.

step one

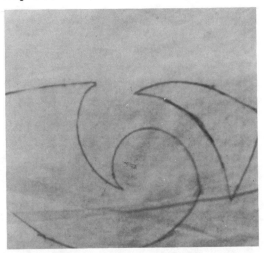

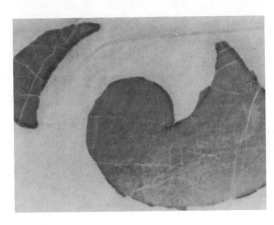

step two

91

RECIPES

Groundnut (Peanut) Soup*

1 tomato
1 potato
1 onion
2 C. water
1 beef bouillon cube
dash salt
1 C. shelled unsalted roasted peanuts
½ C. milk
2 T. rice

Peel and dice the potato and onion. Dice the tomato. Place in a saucepan with water, bouillon cube and salt. Boil for about 30 minutes. Separately, chop the peanuts and combine with the milk. Add the peanut mixture and rice to the saucepan and simmer for 30 minutes. Serve in soup bowls.

Fufu

yams
salt
pepper

Boil peeled yams in a saucepan with salt and pepper until they are soft (about 25 minutes). Let the yams cool, then mash them until soft and free from lumps. Roll the yams into small balls. Serve warm.

Yams are very popular in many African countries. West African yams are different from ours, but you may adapt the recipe with yams or sweet potatoes.

Other foods in Nigeria are:

cassava—the roots are similar to potatoes; the leaves may be used in soups
coco yams
plantains—a type of banana
coconuts
rice

VOCABULARY

(Ibo)

one—*otu*
two—*abuo*
three—*ato*
four—*ano*
five—*ise*
six—*isi*
seven—*asaa*
eight—*asato*
nine—*tolu*
ten—*iri*

Come—*Bia*
Go—*Ga*

Photo by Alma David

Mbabane Swaziland primary school children.

92

KENYA

Color the Kenyan flag.

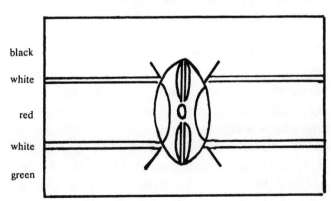

black
white
red
white
green

Can you name these places ?

1. _____.
2. _____.
3. _____.

Answers: Kisumu, Nairobi, Mombasa

93

KENYA

Kenya, a country similar in size to the state of Texas, is located on the eastern coast of Africa and borders the Indian Ocean. Its population is 20,373,000. Ninety-nine percent of the population consists of black Africans, who belong to 50 tribes. The rest are mostly Asians, Arabs, and Europeans.

People from various cultures came to the eastern coast of Africa over a period of many centuries: Egyptian, Greek, and Phoenician explorers; Arab traders; and migrating tribes from central, north and west Africa. Portuguese explorers, European missionaries, Indian traders and British colonists also found their way to East Africa. The Kenyans are descendants of the people from these various cultures.

Europeans developed an interest in East Africa during the 19th century as a result of their need for new markets and raw materials. In 1875 Britain proclaimed itself protector of British East Africa, and seized control of the territory. Kenya became an independent country in 1963. It has a presidential form of government.

The northern three-fifths of the country is barren; and the southern region includes a plateau, ranging from 3,000 to 10,000 feet in altitude, and a low coastal area. Part of the Great Rift Valley extends into Kenya.

Lifestyles in Kenya are primarily modern in the urban areas and ancient in the more remote areas where the people still engage in ancient agricultural practices. Nairobi, the capital, reflects a western and modern lifestyle, whereas Mombasa, the major port and Kenya's second largest city, is Arab in character. It is a popular tourist resort. Other important cities are Kericho, which is known as the "tea capital," and Nakuru, which is a major trading center. Kenyans who live in the cities have a similar lifestyle to that enjoyed by those who live in urban areas in other countries. Kenyans who live in the more remote areas of the country, however, lead a much simpler life. In such areas, many homes are made of thatch and dried mud, and bicycles are a major source of transportation. Also, the market in such areas is often an important place for the bartering of food and other goods as well as a central location for socializing with friends.

In Kenya, students who graduate from primary school but do not continue their education work on the family farms or look for jobs in the cities. Some villages that lack government schools have established their own schools, which are managed and financed locally and which are referred to as "Harambee" schools. In 1977, literacy in the country was 40%. There are two official languages: English and Swahili.

A Kenyan named Keino won international recognition as a famous runner in the 1968 and 1972 Olympic games.

Festival Figures, UNICEF.

CROSSWORD PUZZLE

ACROSS

1. Another word for "us."
4. Grown in Kenya—a drink (not coffee).
5. Kenya is famous for its wild _____.
6. Another word for "also."
7. Kenya's Swahili motto meaning, "Let's all pull together."
11. Kenya is part of this continent.
13. Opposite of "stand."
14. Name of this Eastern African country.
15. Opposite of "cold."

DOWN

1. Kenya's dry areas do not have _____.
2. A United Nations Organization
3. One of Kenya's largest animals.
8. Famous tribe in Kenya.
9. To chew food.
10. Nourishing food Kenyans catch from ponds and the sea.
12. Lion's home.

Reprinted with permission from Country Project Kit on Kenya, UNICEF.

ANSWERS TO PUZZLE

DOWN 1. Water 2. UNICEF 3. Elephant 8. Masai 9. Eat 10. Fish 12. Den

7. *Harambee* 11. Africa 13. Sit 14. Kenya 15. Hot

ACROSS 1. We 4. Tea 5. Animals 6. Too

RECIPES

Samosas*

Samosas are a popular snack in Kenya.

Make a pastry with flour, salt, oil and water. Roll pastry out and cut it into triangles. Be sure the pastry is thin.

Filling:

mincemeat or ground meat
dash of ginger, cinnamon, powdered cloves
2 T. chopped parsley
1 clove garlic, crushed
2 T. water
1 green chili pepper, chopped & seeded
½ C. chopped onion

Saute mincemeat until browned. Add spices and simmer. Stir in onions and parsley. Put a spoonful of the filling on each pastry triangle and fold the triangle over on itself, sealing the edges. Fry the samosas in hot oil until brown.

Irio**

Irio is a dish of the Kikuyu tribe.

3-4 ears of white corn
3-4 potatoes
½ C. dried chick-peas, cooked
water
salt to taste

Boil the corn until the kernels are soft. Cut them from the cob. Put chick-peas and corn in cold water and bring to a boil. Reduce heat and simmer for 2 hours. Add potatoes to separate cooking water and cook until soft. Mash potatoes, corn and peas together and add salt to taste.

This dish may be served with stew or another meat.

VOCABULARY

People in Kenya speak Bantu and Nilotic languages. Bantu means *person*. Bantu is made up of many similar languages. Look how the word "bantu" is sounded out in several of them:

Chewa—ba-nt-u
Ganda—aba-ntu
Kwena—ba-tU
Swahili—wa-tu

Other words from Kenya:

to teach—*xU-rut-a*
teacher—*mU-rut-i*
student—*mU-rut-iw-a*

ISREL

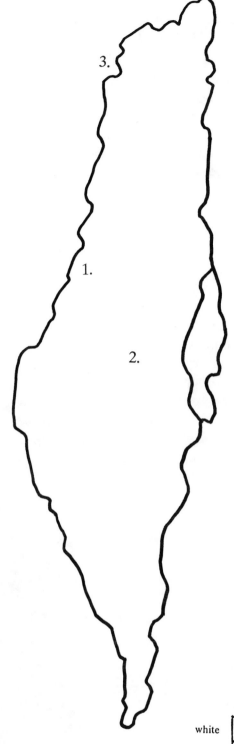

3.

1.

2.

Can you name these places?

1. _____.

2. _____.

3. _____.

Answers: Tel Aviv, Jerusalem, Haifa

Color the Israeli flag.

white

blue

white

blue

white

97

ISRAEL

Israel is a small country in the Middle East. It is about the size of New Jersey. Its neighbors are Lebanon, Syria, Jordan, Saudi Arabia and Egypt. The capital of Israel is Jerusalem. There are beautiful lush green valleys, deserts of sand (called the Negev), tall mountains and areas below sea level. Israel's Dead Sea is so salty that no plants or other living things can grow in it—so salty in fact that it's impossible to sink in it when swimming because the salt holds you up!

Israel is a young country. It was established as a homeland for the Jewish people and was recognized as a nation by the United Nations on May 14, 1948. It is also a holy land for Christians and Moslems. Many of the events recorded in the Bible took place in what is now the country of Israel. The people of Israel came from all over the world seeking religious freedom and escape from persecution and fear.

The people who came to Israel when it was a new country found the land underdeveloped. The entire country virtually had to be built from scratch. These early Israelis were called *Chalutzim* or pioneers. Today, life in Israel is still very hard. Children born in Israel are called *Sabras,* named after the cactus which is hard on the outside and soft and sweet on the inside.

Since the people who come to live in Israel speak many different languages, they are required to learn one: Hebrew, the official language of Israel. The people learn Hebrew in special classes called *Ulpans.* All street signs in Israel are in Hebrew and Arabic. Hebrew is read from right to left and has a completely different alphabet from the English alphabet.

In Israel groups of people sometimes choose to live together in a collection settlement called a *kibbutz.* All the people living in a kibbutz share the work that must be done, and each member of the kibbutz receives food, clothing, medical care and education from the resources of the kibbutz in return. The first kibbutz in Israel, called Oegania, was founded in 1909.

Israel is a land of much variety. It has modern cities, such as Tel Aviv, as well as ancient encampments where Bedouin Arabs live in tents and ride camels. Travelers to Israel can visit ancient Roman ruins, sites of events recorded in the Bible and modern colleges and universities. They can see the national dance of Israel, the *Hora,* performed. Or they can attend a soccer game. Soccer is one of the most popular sports in Israel.

A typical Israeli breakfast includes tomatoes, cucumbers, cheese, eggs and bread. Israelis usually eat their main meal at noon. It usually consists of chicken or fish since there is very little beef in Israel. *Felafel* is a delicious national dish of Israel. It can be bought at felafel stands on street corners.

Most Israeli children start nursery school at age three since both parents usually work outside the home. Children in Israel belong to scouts and other youth groups as they are growing up. They continue their education through high school. The government pays for this schooling. At age 18, every Jewish boy and girl must go into the army. The boys serve three years and the girls serve twenty months. Upon completing their military service, many young people in Israel go to college.

THE HORA

The word *hora* is a Croatian-Serbian word that means "tempo" or "movement." It is a dance of Israel that portrays the flavor of the people. There are variations of steps and melodies; however, the movements follow a basic pattern. All dancers form a single circle and extend both arms to the side so that their hands rest on the shoulders of the people on either side of them. Moving clockwise, step right to the side, place left foot behind the right, and step right. Kick left foot in front of right foot while hopping on the right. Step left to the side, kick right foot across the left while hopping on the left foot. Repeat this pattern. Begin slowly and accelerate.

HAVA NAGILA

A song to sing while you dance the hora.
Ha-va na-gi-la, ha-va na-gi-la, ha-va na-gi-la,
v'-nis-m'-ha.
Ha-va na-gi-la, ha-va na-gi-la, ha-va na-gi-la,
v'-nis-m'-ha.
Ha-va n'-ra'-n'-na, ha-va n'ra'-n'na, ha-va
n'ra'-n'na v'-nis-m'-ha.
Ha-va n'-ra'-n'-na, ha-va n'ra'-n'na, ha-va
n'ra'-n'na v'-nis-m'-ha.
U-ru, u-ru a-him, u-ru a-him b'-lev sa-me-ah,
u-ru a-him, b'lev sa-me-ah,
u-ru a-him, b'lev sa-me-ah,
u-ru a-him, b'lev sa-me-ah,
u-ru a-him, u-ru a-him b'lev sa-me-ah.

Camel made of olive wood from Bethlehem.

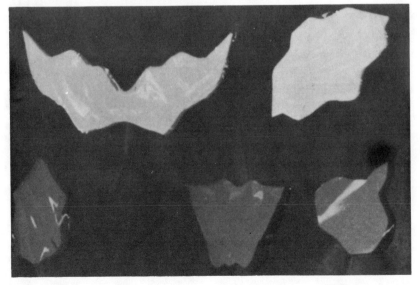

STAINED GLASS WINDOWS

The many synagogues, churches and mosques in Israel have beautiful stained glass windows. You can make windows for your classroom with colored cellophane and black construction paper. Cut out shapes in the paper and tape various colors of cellophane to the back. Put your stained glass window in a window and enjoy the sun shining through.

RECIPES

Felafel

1 packet felafel mix (available at any Greek
    food store)
Pita bread
Sesame Tahini Sauce
Tomatoes, onion, and cucumber finely chopped.

Mix the felafel (a fine powder of ground chick-
peas) according to instructions on package. Warm
pita bread, cut in half, make a pocket, coat pocket
with sauce, insert felafel balls and top with tomatoes,
onion and cucumbers.

Matzo Ball Soup

1 C. matzo meal
½ C. water
4 eggs, beaten
⅓ C. melted shortening
1 t. salt
dash of pepper

Add water, melted shortening, salt and pepper to
the beaten eggs. Mix well. Add matzo meal and
stir thoroughly. Refrigerate 1 hour. Form into
balls and drop into soup or into 1½ quarts boiling
water to which one tablespoon salt has been
added. Cook 20 minutes.

Dates

In Israel, dates are popular at holiday seasons
and are used for desserts. Date palm trees grow
mainly in desert lands. When the dates are ripe,
they droop from the tree and hang in heavy bunches.
The sweet dates can be eaten by themselves or
added to other dessert recipes.

VOCABULARY

one—*achet*
two—*shtayim*
three—*shalosh*
four—*arba*
five—*chamash*
six—*shesh*
seven—*sheva*
eight—*shmone*
nine—*tesha*
ten—*eser*

Hello or good-bye—
    Shalom (peace)
Mother—*Abba*
Father—*Imma*
dog—*kelev*
cat—*chatul*
house—*bayit*

THE HEBREW ALPHABET

NAME SOUND	HEBREW NAME	LETTER	NAME SOUND	HEBREW NAME	LETTER
Alef silent	אָלֶף	א	final Mem M	מֵם סוֹפִית	ם
Bet B	בֵּית	ב	Nun N	נוּן	נ
Vet V	בֵית	כ	final Nun N	נוּן סוֹפִית	ן
Gimel G(get)	גִמֶל	ג	Sameh S	סָמֶך	ס
Dalet D	דָלֶת	ד	Ayin silent	עָיִן	ע
Hay H	הֵא	ה	Pay P	פָּא	פ
Vav V	וָו	ו	Fay F	פָא	פ
Zayin Z	זַיִן	ז	final Fay F	פָא סוֹפִית	ף
Het H	חִית	ח	Tzadee TZ	צָדִי	צ
Tet T	טִית	ט	final Tzadee TZ	צָדִי סוֹפִית	ץ
Yod Y	יוֹד	י	Kof K	קוֹף	ק
Kaf K	כָּף	כ	Resh R	רֵישׁ	ר
Haf H	כָף	כ	Shin SH	שִׁין	שׁ
final Haf H	כָף סוֹפִית	ך	Sin S	שִׂין	שׂ
Lamed L	לָמֶד	ל	Tav T	תָּו	ת
Mem M	מֵם	מ	Tav T	תָו	ת

EGYPT

Can you name these places?

1. _____ .

2. _____ .

3. _____ .

Color the Egyptian flag.

red

white

yellow
emblem

black

101

Egypt is located on the northern coast of Africa with the Mediterranean Sea to its north and the Sahara desert to the south. Egypt, the land of the pharoahs, is one of the world's oldest civilized lands in the world - its history extends to 5000 years before the birth of Christ. It has a population of more than 45 million people. Most Egyptians live in the towns and villages along the Nile River Valley. The desert constitutes 96% of the land area of Egypt and supports 4% of the population.

The climate ranges from mild winters to summer temperatures which may go as high as 135 degrees farenheit in Upper Egypt. Egypt has gone four years without rain.

Egypt attracts many tourists. There are many historical sites to see, including the Great Pyramids. These massive structures have endured as lasting monuments to ancient rulers and to the civilization which conceived and built them. The Great Pyramid, or Pyramid of Khufu (Cheops), was built by 100,000 men over a period of 20 years. The early Egyptians had a profound belief in immortality. By 2700 B.C. they were embalming the dead and building elaborate stone tombs shaped as pyramids for burial of the pharoah. The Valley of the Kings lies on the west bank of the Nile, across from Luxor. The rulers of the 18th, 19th, and 20th Dynasties prepared tombs carved out of the underground rock. The smallest but most famous of the tombs in the Valley is that of King Tutankhamen, known as King Tut. The maginificent treasures of King Tut, housed in the Cairo Museum, were found by Howard Carter, a British archeologist, in 1922, after 7 seasons of examining the area.

Egypt is one of the most modern, yet traditional, Arab states. Many women still wear the long black garments with veils to cover their faces. They still carry burdens on their heads. In larger cities, women dressed in western style clothing can be seen along with women who cling to the past. Much has been done to educate the children, create better housing for the poor, and provide free medical services. Arabic is the official language of the country. It is written and read right to left. Books are read back to front. Hieroglyphics is a system of writing used in ancient Egypt in which pictures are used to represent sounds, words, or ideas. The Hieroglyphic code was broken by a French officer of engineers when the Rosetta Stone was found near Alexandria in 1799. The cartouche, an oval shape around a name written in hieroglyphics, denotes royalty.

Cairo, the capital, is situated on the northern end of the Nile River. As in other large cities, there is a lot of noise from the cars and bustle of city life. The small, rural towns are scattered throughout Egypt and are much quieter. But even in the most modern towns, one can always count on seeing a camel or two.

Education has become a major concern for Egyptians. Boys and girls between the ages of six twelve are required to go to school. Many continue their education after high school and attend colleges and universities in Cairo and around the world. New schools are being opened in the desert to curb population density in Cairo. The curriculum of preparatory and secondary schools is becoming more diversified with foreign language and vocational studies becoming increasingly important. The children go to school six days a week. Friday, the Moslem sabbath, is like Sunday in the United States. All children study the usual courses: mathematics, geography, science, grammar, history, etc., but they also take religion classes so they can better understand their religion, Islam. Islam is the official religion of Egypt and is an important part of the Egyptian life, since Moslems follow the Koran (the Moslem holy book) and use the laws of the Koran to govern their lives.

VOCABULARY

School — *Med-ressa*
How are you? — *Keef-Halek*
Fine — *Bahee*
Thank you — *Shook-ran*
Goodbye (Literal translation: Peace be with you)
— *Ma-ai Saalama*

one—*waahid*
two—*aθneen*
three—*θalaaθa*
four—*arbaʕ*
five—*xamsa*
six—*sitta*
seven—*sab9a*
eight—*θamaanya*
nine—*tis9a*
ten—*9asǎra*

You are welcome!
'Ahlan wa sahlan!

How are you?
Šloonak?

Fine, thanks.
Bxeer maškuur.

GAMES

— Hop Scotch
— A modified version of Jacks (They substitute marbles for Jacks)
— Soccer is Egypt's favorite sport, both to play and watch.
— Egyptians enjoy watching television, especially American detective shows and cartoons.

North African camel

RECIPES

Cous Cous   Serves 4

All ingredients can be found at a gourmet food shop.

1 box cous cous
1 chicken (cut up)
½ cup olive or corn oil
4 large onions, chopped
Salt to taste
Pepper, red, to taste
1 t. cumin powder
½ can tomato paste
1 can homos (chickpeas)
2 potatoes, chopped
4 carrots, chopped
3 zucchinis, chopped
1 t. cinnamon

Put the oil in a deep pot and heat. When hot, add the onions and saute. Then add the tomato paste, pepper, cumin and salt. Stir until mixed with oil and onions, then add the chicken. Add 5 cups of water and let simmer for a few minutes. Then taste to see if more salt or other spices need to be added. Add vegetables. Let cook until chicken is done.

In the meantime, start to prepare the cous cous. Follow directions on the box. When cous cous has been cooked, place on a large platter and add cinnamon to it. Stir it in. Then top with the sauce and the meat and vegetables. Do not put all the sauce on at once unless you like it soupy.

Serve with radishes on the side.

Soup   Serves 6

1 lb. lamb, cut into cubes
1 large onion, chopped
2 T. tomato paste
2 T. oil
1 bunch parsley, chopped
1 tomato, chopped
1 lemon
½ t. each of salt, pepper, red pepper, turmeric
½ can chickpeas
3 T. shorba pasta (orzo)
1 T. dry mint (optional)

Place pot on low flame; add lamb and onions. When onions are soft add the 2 T. oil, stir and cover. Add the tomato paste, half the parsley and the chopped tomato; stir. Add the juice of ½ the lemon, salt, pepper, red pepper, and turmeric. Add 1 cup water. Cover and cook about 15 minutes. Add the rest of the parsley, cover and cook for a few minutes. Then add 3 more cups of water and cook another 15 minutes. Add ½ can of chickpeas and the shorba pasta. Cook 10 minutes or until lamb and shorba pasta are done.

To serve: Put soup in individual bowls and sprinkle dried mint on top.

NOTE:
Shorba pasta is a tiny pasta similar in shape and size to a grain of rice. Orzo is the Greek name, and it can be bought under this name in the United States.

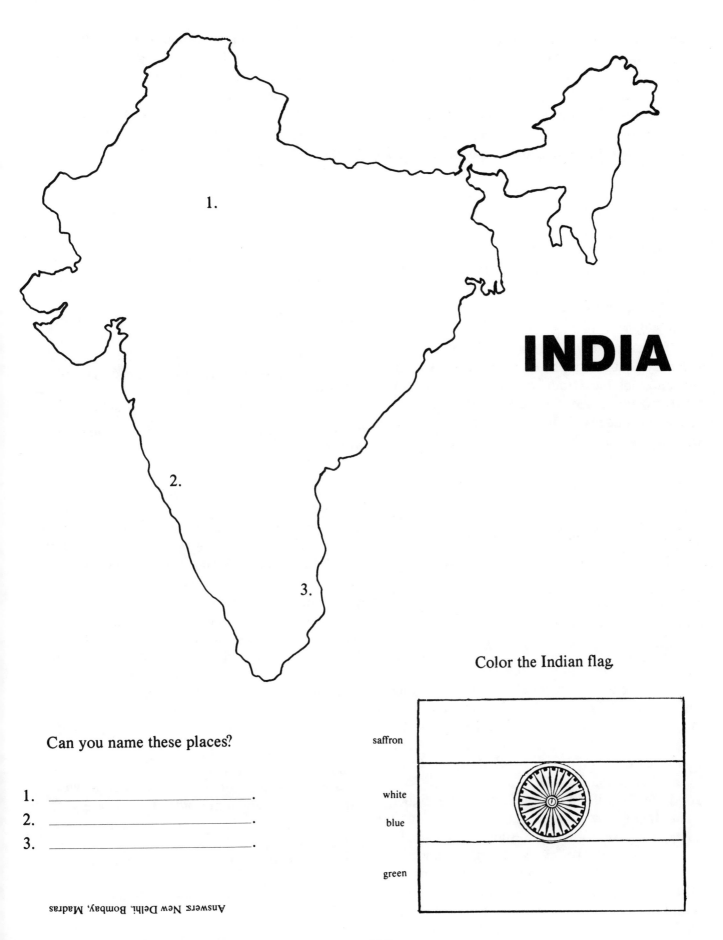

INDIA

1.

2.

3.

Color the Indian flag.

saffron

white

blue

green

Can you name these places?

1. _____.

2. _____.

3. _____.

INDIA

India is a country that is 4500 years old. It is a peninsula in South Asia. With more than 800 million people, India is second only to China in world population. In the recent past, It was part of the British Empire. Mahatma Gandhi led the struggle for India's independence from Britain, and in 1947 India became a free and independent country. Today, it is the largest democracy in the world. People vote every five years to choose their representatives. The first prime minister was Nehru Gandhi, who was later succeeded by his daughter, Indira Gandhi. In 1984, she was assassinated and the ruling party chose her son, Rajiv, to succeed her. In 1989, he lost the elections and now the prime minister is V.P. Singh.

Indian society is set up in a rigidly-defined *caste* system. This caste system results from teachings of the Hindu religion, which is the predominant religion in India. Islam is another religion practiced in India. In India, each person is born into a particular caste or class. A person's lifestyle, language, customs and beliefs are determined by his caste. Loyalty among members of a caste is very strong. There is very little social interaction betwen castes, and marriages between members of different castes are extremely rare.

The highest caste is the BRAHMIN. Other castes include the KSHATRIYA, VAISYA, SHUDRA and HARIJAN, the lowest caste (formerly known as the Untouchables).

Whatever caste a person is born into is his caste for life; it is impossible for an Indian to move from one caste to another— at least during this lifetime. An aspect of the Hindu religion that is most important to the Indian people is the belief in *reincarnation.* Hindu Indians believe that when a person dies his soul returns to earth in another living form. If a person has lived a good life, he will be reincarnated into a higher caste. If not, he will be reincarnated into a lower caste or a lower form of life, such as an animal.

Because they believe so strongly in reincarnation, many people in India are vegetarians. In addition, you will often see cows and other animals wandering freely in the streets of India. These things occur because the Indian people believe animals may be reincarnated souls.

Hindi is becoming the offical language of India along with the native languages of the country. There are thirteen regional languages in India, such as Tamil, Telugu, Urdu and Bengali. More than 100 dialects are spoken in India. Because the British ruled India for many years, you also hear English spoken frequently. It is taught in the Indian schools, so most educated Indians can speak English.

The capital of India is New Delhi. Another interesting place is Agra, the location of the famous Taj Mahal. The Taj Mahal is a mausoleum which the Shahjahan, a ruler of India, built as a monument of love to his third wife, who died bearing his fourteenth child. Varanasi is the oldest active city in the world. It is also the holiest city in India. The Ganges, a holy river, flows through Varanasi. Hindus bathe in this holy river and many desire to be cremated at the Manikarnika Ghat when they die so that their ashes may be thrown into the river.

The women in India wear an item of clothing called a *sari.* A sari is a piece of cloth six yards long and fory-five inches wide. Usually the women wear a short blouse and a half-slip with a tight waistband under the sari.

This is how an Indian woman wears a sari: she tucks one end of the fabric into the front waistband of her slip and wraps it around her hip to the left. She brings it to the front, gathers six to twelve small pleats down the front and tucks them into her waistband. She wraps the sari around her again until it reaches the front. She then throws the remaining cloth over her left shoulder and pins it in place.

India has beautiful art, music and handicrafts. Coconut fiber mats, silk carpets from Kashmir, splendid bronze statuettes, woodblock printing, weaving and needlework (done with gold threads), and embroidery work are just some of the handicrafts produced in India. Indian cooking is delicious. It depends a lot on the use of spices for its unique flavor, such as cardamon, pepper, cinnamon, coriander, cumin, fenugreek, mustard, clove, nutmeg, mace, saffron, turmeric, garlic, ginger, onion and vanilla.

GAMES

Backgammon, parcheesi and chess are believed to have originated in India.

Create A Shadow Puppet

It is believed the Shadow Play was born in India. The performance of the legendary story, Ramayana, is a favorite in India. This Hindu epic is a story of an Indian Rama who conquers evil forces. The people admire the good King Rama, a protector of the weak and poor. They respect the purity of his Queen, Sita.

You can create your puppet with cardboard or tagboard, a needle, tape, scissors, string, crayons or paint and some brads. Draw the parts of the puppet's body and cut them out. Punch holes in the arms, legs, and head and attach them with brads to the puppet's torso. Tape a stick to the puppet's back. Tie strings to each body part and tape the string to the stick or an overhead bar. Pull the strings to move the body parts.

Shiva, the embodiment of Good, the Cosmic Dancer.

Ganesha, the remover of obstacles, is the son of Shiva.

RECISE

RECIPES

Puris
(Flat, round, whole wheat bread)
2 T. butter
1 C. water
2 C. whole wheat flour, sifted
dash of salt
oil for frying
Mix flour and salt. Cut in butter and add water until dough is soft. Form a ball and let sit about 1 hour. Knead and shape dough into small balls. Roll out into five inch rounds. Be sure they are thin. Fry, browning both sides.

These puris can be served with other dishes.

Chicken Curry*
4 onions, chopped
¼ C. butter
3 pounds chicken
3 T. curry powder
dash salt
2 C. water
1 T. lemon juice
Saute onion in butter. Add meat and saute 10 more minutes. Add curry and cook until chicken is browned. Add water and salt,, cover and simmer about 40 minutes. Add lemon juice. Serve over rice.

NOTE: You may substitute cubed meat, fish or shellfish for the chicken.

Vegetable samosas and mutton kabobs are popular north Indian snacks. Lassi(a drink made of yogurt) is a favorite Panjabi drink.

VOCABULARY

Hello — *Namaste*
Thank you — *Dhanyavad*
Traditional dress for women — *Sari*

one—*ek*
two—*do*
three—*teen*
four—*char*
five—*panch*
six—*chay*
seven— *saat*
eight— *aath*
nine—*nau*
ten—*das*

Indira Gandhi, a former Prime Minister of India

EUROPE

Germany boys on holiday.

Little Mermaid, Copenhagen

1.

2.

3.

SPAIN

Can you name these places?

1. _____.

2. _____.

3. _____.

Color the Spanish flag.

red

yellow

red

black, red, green emblem

SPAIN

Spain is the third largest European country after Russia and France. It occupies most of the Iberian Penninsula which it shares with Portugal. Spain also includes the Canary Islands and the Balearic Islands. France lies to the east of Spain and Africa lies only ten miles south of Spain, across the Strait of Gibraltar.

Spain has increased its economic development since the mid-1900's. Chemical products, shoes and clothing are also manufactured. Because of the increase in manufacturing and construction industries in Spain, many Spaniards have left the traditional occupation of farming. Farming is still an important industry in Spain, however. Farm products from Spain include olives, oranges, wheat and wine grapes.

In Spain, the King is head of state. He appoints the prime minister, the president and members of parliament. The King also represents Spain at diplomatic and ceremonial affairs. The governor of each of Spain's fifty provinces is appointed by the national government. The people of each province elect the members of a provincial assembly.

The official language of Spain is Castilian Spanish. Pronunciation varies slightly from area to area.

Madrid is Spain's capital and its largest city. One of the most famous art museums in the world, the Prado, lies in the heart of Madrid. It contains thousands of oil paintings, etchings, and sculptures. Works of Goya, Rubens, Velaquez, El Greco and Titian, among others, are exhibited in the Prado. Madrid also has many beautiful gardens and parks, among them the Botanical Garden founded in 1781 by Charles III. El Escorial, the burial place of Spanish kings and queens, is northwest of Madrid. The monumental Valle de los Caidos, a memorial to Spain's Civil War dead, is close to El Escorial. It is an extraordinary architectural achievement: a crypt, cut through 853 feet of solid rock, and surmounted by a 492 foot cross of concrete faced with stone. Another well-known spot in Madrid is the Plaza Mayor where bullfights are held. Bullfighting is a popular sport in Spain.

Spain has many other historical and interesting cities. For instance, Barcelona is Spain's largest port and second largest city. In 1493, Isabella and Ferdinand, King and Queen of Spain, welcomed Columbus home from the New World at this port city. Today, the *Santa Maria,* Columbus' flagship, stands just right of a bronze statue, the Admiral of the Ocean Monument, in Barcelona. Another important Spanish city is Segovia, famous for its castles, Romanesque architecture and a Roman aqueduct. The aqueduct is one of the best preserved Roman ruins in the world and, in fact, is still in use. Avila is a city enclosed by a wall. It was featured in the movie, *The Pride and the Passion.* Granada is famous for the Alhambra, a moorish palace. It is also the site of a famous battle between the Moors and Ferdinand of Spain in 1492 which marked the beginning of the end of Moorish rule in Spain.

FIESTAS: HOLIDAYS IN SPAIN

The Festival Of Semana Santa (Holy Week) is celebrated in many towns, but the celebration in Seville is world famous. The people of Seville hold torchlight processions in which marchers wearing costumes which originated as far back as the fifteenth century carry aloft statues of the Virgin Mary and the Catholic saints. The boys dress in penitent clothing, monklike robes that are black, white, green or purple, and wear peaked hats and masks.

Feria De Sevilla (Seville Fair) is held in the spring after Holy Week. The street of a section of the city is decorated and booths are set up for the sale of food and drink. Music, singing, dancing and laughter are continuous for seven days.

Running Of The Bulls takes place in Pambalone each year. This is the town where the bulls for the bullfights are raised. The bulls are let out in the streets and the people chase them—or get chased!

Alcazar, the castle featured in the movie Camelot   Photo by C.T. Caballero

113

RECIPES

Paella

Yellow paella rice (found in most grocery stores)
Frozen or canned fish: shrimp, oysters, clams, sardines, etc.
Leftover chicken or pork
Garlic salt
Mushrooms (canned or fresh)
Peas (optional)
Stuffed green olives
Cook rice as directed. Place in baking dish with other ingredients. Cook until completely heated.

The Spanish serve paella with lemon wedges and shellfish on top. Garlic bread adds to the meal.

Leche Frita (Fried Custard Squares)

½ C. cornstarch
3 C. milk
½ c. plus 2 T. sugar
2 eggs, slightly beaten
1 C. fine bread crumbs, trimmed of crusts
4 T. butter
2 T. oil
1 t. cinnamon

In a 2 quart saucepan, combine cornstarch and 1 cup of milk and stir until the cornstarch dissolves. Stir in the remaining milk and ½ cup sugar. Bring to a boil over high heat, stirring constantly until the mixture thickens. Pour into a shallow 9 inch baking dish. Spread evenly and refrigerate for 4 hours. Cut into squares. Dip the squares into the beaten eggs and then into the crumbs. Place on sheet of waxed paper. Melt butter in the oil and brown the squares on each side. Sprinkle with cinnamon and sugar. EAT!

VOCABULARY

English words borrowed from Spanish.

fiesta
enchilada
tamale
chili con carne
rodeo
bronco
mustang
lariat
mesa
arroyo
canyon
coyote
patio
plaza
adobe
guerilla
armada
mosquito
embargo

Bullfighter in the Plaza Mayor.

Photo by C.T. Caballero.

114

ITALY

Adriatic Sea

Tyrrhenian Sea

Mediterranean Sea

Ionian Sea

3.

2.

1.

Color the Italian flag.

green	white	red

Can you name these places?

1. _____.
2. _____.
3. _____.

Answers: Sicily, Rome, Alps

115

ITALY

Italy is a long, narrow peninsula shaped like a boot that lies in the center of the Mediterranean Sea. Sardinia, one of its two islands, is off the knee of the boot, opposite Italy's capital, Rome. The other island, Sicily, is close to the toe, not far from North Africa.

There are many mountains in Italy. The Alps rise along the top edge of the boot and form a wall between Italy and her neighbors. The highest mountain in Europe, Mont Blanc, forms the border between Italy and France. The Alps have beautiful lakes, created by glaciers. The Apennine mountains run down the whole length of Italy and appear again in Sicily. Italy's two live volcanoes, Mount Etna in Sicily, and Mount Vesuvius near the Bay of Naples, are part of this range. When one of these volcanoes erupts, many buildings collapse and wide cracks appear in the ground. Because of these volcanoes, parts of Italy have been rising and falling for centuries. Italy also has lowlands which stretch from the hills to the sea. The famous beaches of the Italian Riviera are only slender strips of pebbles in the northwestern corner of Italy. The only big valley in Italy is just south of the Alps where the Po River and its branches have flattened out an area one sixth the size of the whole country.

The villages among the hills may be squeezed in between cliffs. The roads twist and turn up the mountains. Living space is cramped in Italy because of the large population (over 50 million people).

Italy has few natural resources. Mercury and sulfur are the only minerals in the country. The forests have been cut down over the years and the soil is poor. Rainfall is limited. With little to live on, survival is a matter of the ability to grow and make things for the people in this small crowded land.

The people of Italy are of mixed descent and so have inherited their looks, their ways of life, and their special skills from many different ancestors. Italy is famous for its pottery. Italian potters often use ancient Etruscan designs. The sailors in Italy's navy are heirs to an old tradition. The Phoenicians, who came to Italy many years ago, were the greatest sea traders and navigators of their time. The New World was even discovered by an Italian, Christopher Columbus, who grew up in the port city of Genoa. The stone masons of Italy learned their art from the columned temples erected more than two thousand years ago by the Romans. The Romans had learned to build their temples from Greeks of even earlier times. Modern Italian roads are among the best in the world because Italians have been building roads since the time of the Roman Empire. Many of the Roman roads are still in use today. For example, the Via Appia (Appian Way) was first paved in 312 B.C.

Italy's most important industry is the metal industry. Thousands of people work in plants that manufacture small machines, such as typewriters, sewing machines, and aircraft equipment. Many workers in various parts of Italy create leather shoes, gloves, and handbags. Most farming is done in the fertile Po Valley. Farmers grow grain, sugar beets, peach and apple orchards and vegetables. They also grow the popular artichoke and the finocchi, a licorice-tasting plant, in the Po Valley.

All Italians are proud of the past that they share, but various segments of the Italian population are also proud of the things that differenciate them from Italians in other parts of the country. In the north, the people can travel to other parts of Europe. Many are modern, businesslike and efficient. They may have light hair and blue eyes. The southern Italians have had to adapt to a very different climate. They have learned to live under a hot sun and strong winds from the Sahara Desert. In this part of the country, where the Greeks, the Phoenicians, and the dark-skinned Arabs once ruled, most people have black hair and dark eyes.

The State of Vatican City is the smallest independent country in the world. It is a tiny walled city inside the city of Rome. It covers 108 acres. Its ruler is the Pope of the Roman Catholic Church. The Vatican has about a thousand citizens. The Roman Catholic Religion is the major religion in Italy.

Gondolas are long, flat-bottomed boats with tall ornamental stems and sterns which are used for transportation on the canals in Venice. The gondolier (pictured here) poles or rows the gondola with a long pole.

117

GAMES OF ITALY

Soccer is the most important sport in Italy. During the major league soccer season, from September through May, thousands of excited fans fill the stadiums all over the country. Italian boys play sandlot soccer, just as American boys play sandlot baseball.

Bicycle racing is also very popular. Boys begin practicing very early so that someday they may be able to enter the famous Golden Wheel race held every July in Bergamo.

Follow Through Tag is another popular game. Ten to twenty players may participate. They form a circle, clasping hands and holding their arms up to make arches. One player, the runner, stands inside the circle while another, the chaser, stands outside. The chaser tries to catch the runner, but he must follow the runner's route exactly. New players are chosen when the runner is caught.

The *Tarentella* is a traditional dance performed in Italy. It is danced at parties, weddings, and other get-togethers. The women lift their full skirts slightly and do a skipping motion around their partners.

MUSICAL INSTRUMENTS*

See if you can recognize the instruments of the orchestra. Many of the words used in the symphony orchestra were taken from the Italian language. (See Vocabulary next page.)

Orchestra Instruments

String Family
Bass Viol
Cello
Viola
Violin

Woodwind
Piccolo
Flute
Clarinet
English Horn
Oboe
Bassoon

Percussion
Kettle Drum
Chimes
Cymbals
Snare Drum
Triangle

Brass
Trumpet
Tuba
French horn
Trombone

*Reprinted with permission from THE HANDBOOK OF LEARNING ACTIVITIES FOR YOUNG CHILDREN, J. Caballero, Humanics Limited, Atlanta.

118

RECIPES

Spaghetti

1 medium onion, chopped
1 green pepper, chopped
clove garlic
ground beef, 1 pound
½ t. chili pepper
⅓ can tomato paste
Parmesan cheese
1 can mushrooms
4 T. ketchup
chopped ripe, stuffed olives
olive oil
2 T. butter
1 box spaghetti noodles, cooked

Saute onions and garlic, add meat. Add other ingredients and simmer for a while. Pour over spaghetti and serve.

Lasagna

Cook lasagna noodles (8oz. box) in 4 cups water. Prepare the following mixture:

2 T. olive oil
1-2 lbs. ground beef
1 T. garlic
¾ C. onion
1 6oz. can tomato paste
1 can tomato sauce
tomatoes (optional)
dash salt, oregano, basil and pepper

Alternate the following:

Noodles
Meat mixture
Mozarella cheese (approximately 1 lb.)
Ricotta (cottage) cheese (1 carton)

Bake at 350 degrees for 1 hour.

Mini Pizza

½ English muffin
1 T. tomato sauce (see below)
1 T. grated cheese

Sauce:
1 6oz. can tomato paste
½ C. water
garlic salt

Spread tomato sauce on the muffin. Sprinkle with cheese. Broil for about 5 minutes.

VOCABULARY

English words which come from the Italians:

> *cello*
> *opera*
> *operetta*
> *finale*
> *soprano*
> *contralto*
> *concerto*
> *pasta*
> *pizza*
> *spaghetti*
> *salami*
> *ravioli*
> *spumoni*
> *mostoccioli*
> *gondola*
> *confetti*
> *parasol*
> *portico*
> *influenza*
> *malaria*

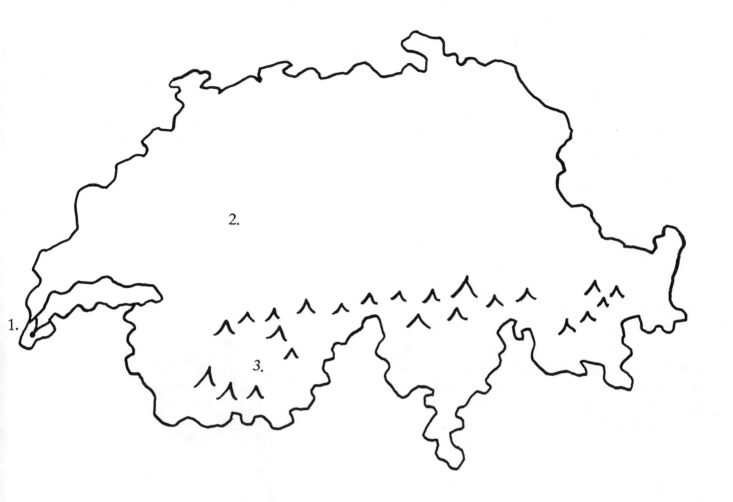

SWITZERLAND

Can you name these places?

1. _____.
2. _____.
3. _____.

Color the Swiss flag.

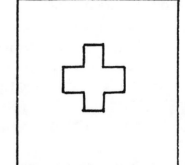

red
field

white
cross

SWITZERLAND

Switzerland is a land of lakes, mountains and lush green pastures, modern cities and old-world villages. It is a very peaceful country. In the summer, it is exciting to take steamer trips on the beautiful lakes and climb the mountains by cable car. A visitor can learn to play an *alpenhorn* like the men of the mountains, and enjoy watching the cows, adorned with flower necklaces, return to their farms for the winter. Swiss folk dances are fun to watch and are very popular.

Zurich is a modern commercial area with beautiful lakes filled with swans and sailboats. Mountains and chateaus are only a short distance away. It is a popular tourist spot because of the beautiful scenery.

Geneva is surrounded on three sides by France, so it may remind you of France. Geneva is an international city and hosts many world organizations and international conferences and conventions. It is a beautiful city and many people from other countries decide to live there.

Bern is the capial of Switzerland. It is located on a plateau that runs across the middle of the country between two mountain ranges. Most of the population of Switzerland is centered in this area.

Switzerland has three official languages: German, French and Italian. It has limited natural resources, but is a thriving industrial nation. The Swiss import most of their raw materials, but manufacture electrical equipment, machinery and watches. Swiss watches are renowned .
The Swiss also produce large quantities of cheese, chocolate and other dairy products.

The government is democratic and is built on the Swiss Constitution of 1848. Switzerland also has complete freedom of religion. Approximately half of the people are Protestant and half are Roman Catholic.

Children must attend school from age six to fourteen. Switzerland has numerous trade and technical schools and seven universities.

Swiss literature is written in German. Two of the most famous Swiss books are *Swiss Family Robinson* by the Wyss family and *Heidi* by Johanna Spyri.

GAMES

Kick the Can

The children play this game outdoors. Three to ten players are needed. One person is chosen to be "it". He stands near a can that has been placed on the ground. He then covers his eyes and counts to ten while the others run and hide. Then "it" runs to find the others. When "it" finds a player, that player tries to make it back to the can before "it" can tag him. The first player to get tagged becomes "it." If all the players make it back to the can safely, then "it" must be "it" again.

ACTIVITY

Draw a watercolor mountain. You will need tissues or napkins and watercolors. Wet the paper and then apply the tissue to form mountain shapes. Use watercolors to define the outline. The texture of mountains will result when the paint bleeds through the tissue. Fill in the rest of the picture with watercolor wash while the paper is wet. A person, house or trees may be added, if desired.*

* Reprinted with permission from ART PROJECTS FOR YOUNG CHILDREN, J. Caballero, Humanics Limited, 1980.

RECIPES

Cheese Fondue

½ C. cheddar cheese
½ C. Cheese Whiz

Melt the cheese in a fondue pot. Dip one inch cubes of French bread into the cheese.

Swiss cheese with a dash of garlic may be substituted.

Mini-meatballs

½ lb. ground beef, cooked
1 egg, beaten
2 T. evaporated milk
3 T. cracker crumbs
dash salt
dash pepper
2 T. grated onion

Combine the cooked meat with the other ingredients. Shape into small meatballs. Chill. Dip into hot oil fondue.

Sauces can be made of Heinz, Worchestershire, ketchup, mustard, or horseradish.

Chocolate Fondue

Chocolate sauce
Powdered sugar
Coconut
Fruit

Heat the chocolate sause in a fondue pot. Dip the fruits into the sauce, then into the coconut or sugar. NOTE: Dip the fruits into lemon juice before serving to prevent them from darkening.

Draw a mountain climber climbing the Matterhorn.

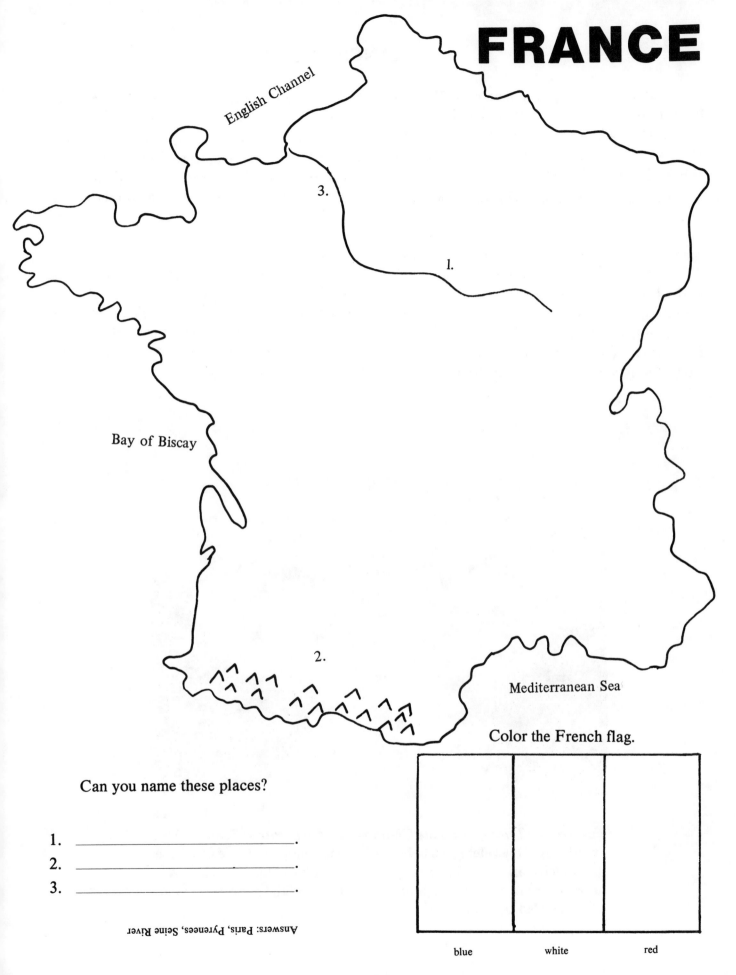

FRANCE

English Channel

3.

1.

Bay of Biscay

2.

Mediterranean Sea

Color the French flag.

Can you name these places?

1. _____.
2. _____.
3. _____.

Answers: Paris, Pyrenees, Seine River

| blue | white | red |

125

FRANCE

France is the largest country in Western Europe. It ranks second only to Russia in land area among all the European nations. France is about twice the size as the state of Colorado. It has a population of over 55 million people.

France is a beautiful and historic country. It has areas with snow-capped Alps, sunny beaches in the south, picturesque fishing villages, and spacious wooded valleys. Colorful apple orchards, dairy farms and vineyards lie throughout much of the French countryside.

French children between the ages of six and sixteen attend school. The Ministry of National Education decides on the curriculum and how it shall be taught. Children between the ages of two and six may choose to attend a free nursery school. France has a literacy rate of 97%.

France became industrialized during the second half of the nineteenth century. Today, it is one of the world's major industrial and agricultural countries. It has many natural resources, including coal, iron ore, bauxite, potash and sulfur. It is a principle producer of agricultural and fishery products.

Family life is very important in France. The French holidays are tied closely to the Roman Catholic Church. *Noel* (Christmas) is marked by family reunions and celebration. On *Paques* (Easter), children receive candy much like children do in the United States.

Photo by C.T. Caballero.

The Arch de Triomphe on the Champes Elysee in Paris. Bastille Day, July 14, is being celebrated to honor France's independence day—the day which marks the anniversary of the beginning of the French Revolution, which resulted in the people's overthrow of the oppressive monarchy headed by Louis XVI.

126

FRENCH SONGS

Sing these favorite songs from France with your children.

FRERE JACQUES

Fre-re Jac-ques, Fre-re Jac-ques, Dor-mez vous?
Dor-mez vous?
Are you sleeping? Are you sleeping? Brother
John. Brother John.

Sonnez-les ma-ti-nes. Son-nez les ma-ti-nes.
Morning bells are ringing. Morning bells are
ringing.

Din don din. Din don din.
Ding Dong Ding. Ding Dong Ding.

WHERE IS THUMBKIN?

1. *Where is Thumb-kin? Where is Thumb-kin?*
   Here I am, Here I am.
   How are you to-day, Sir?
   Very well, I thank you.
   Run a-way, run a-way.
2. *Pointer*
3. *Tall Man*
4. *Ring Man*
5. *Pink-y*

Actions: Put both hands behind your back. When you say, "Here I am" bring the right, then left hand forward, holding up the correct finger. When you say, "How are you..." wiggle each finger, as if the two fingers were talking to each other.

RECIPES

Crepes

2 eggs
⅔ C. milk
1 T. melted shortening
½ C. sifted all-purpose flour
¼ t. salt
dash of sugar

Beat eggs. Add milk and shortening. Sift flour, salt and sugar together and add to eggs. Beat until smooth. Drop batter on greased crepe griddle. Cook until brown. Turn once.

You may fill your crepe with almost anything: meats such as roast beef or hamburger; vegetables such as squash or broccoli; or desserts such as chocolate chips or fresh fruits.

Quiche

1 9" pie shell
12 bacon slices
4 eggs
2 C. heavy cream
dash salt, nutmeg, sugar, pepper
1 C. Swiss cheese

Heat oven to 425 degrees. Fry and crumble bacon. Beat together other ingredients, except cheese. Sprinkle pie shell with cheese and bacon. Pour mixture on top. Bake at 425 degrees 15 minutes. Reduce heat to 300 degrees and bake for 40 minutes. To test for doneness, insert a knife in the middle of the quiche. If it comes out clean, the quiche is done.

French Dressing

¼ C. salad oil
½ C. sugar
¾ C. vinegar
1 can tomato soup
1 t. salt
1 clove garlic

Combine all ingredients and blend well. Pour dressing on salad.

VOCABULARY

one—*un*
two—*deux*
three—*trois*
four—*quatre*
five—*cinq*
six—*six*
seven—*sept*
eight—*huit*
nine—*neuf*
ten—*dix*

Two heads are better than one.
Deux avis valent mieux qu'un.

It is six of one and half a dozen of the other.
C'est bonnet blan et blanc bonnet.

A friend in need is a friend indeed.
C'est dans le besoin qu'on connait ses amis.

NETHERLANDS

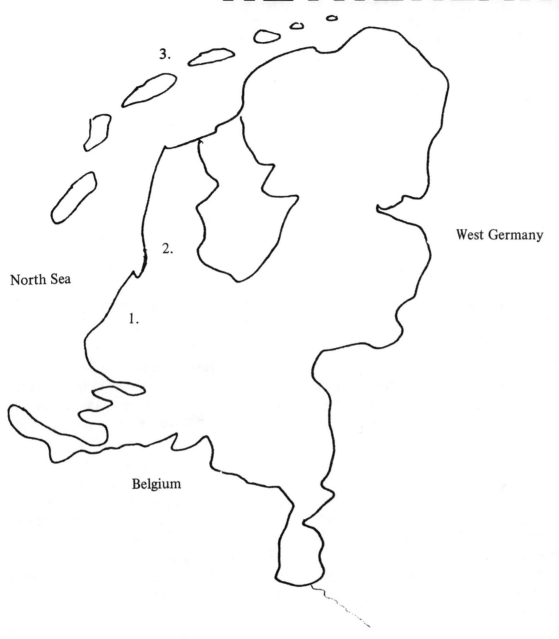

3.

North Sea

2.

1.

West Germany

Belgium

Can you name these places?

1. _____.
2. _____.
3. _____.

Answers: The Hague, Amsterdam, West Frisian Islands

Color the Dutch flag.

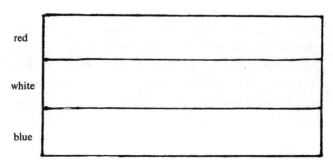

red

white

blue

129

THE NETHERLANDS

The Netherlands, also known as Holland, is a country located in northwestern Europe. Its neighbors to the south and east are Belgium and Germany, and the North Sea surrounds it on the north and west. Most of the land in Holland is low and flat. In fact, Holland, Luxembourg and Belgium are called the Low Countries. The Netherlands is also sometimes called the land of water. The people who live in the Netherlands or Holland are called the Dutch.

Amsterdam is the capital of Holland. Amsterdam was the city in which the Frank family, who were Jewish, went into hiding from the Nazis during World War II. They spent over two years in a secret attic in a building in Amsterdam. Anne Frank, who was thirteen when the family first moved to the secret attic, wrote a famous diary of her life while in hiding there.

Since the altitude of the land in Holland is so very low and since the country is almost surrounded by the North Sea, the Dutch people had to construct *dikes* along the shoreline and along the banks of the many canals which extend inland from the sea into Holland to prevent flooding and destruction of their land. To construct a dike, the people first built a core of packed sand. Then they covered the sand with heavy clay, and then planted grass with long roots on top. Finally, they strengthened the side of the dike facing the water by reinforcing it with logs of wood and large blocks of stone.

The Dutch use wind as a source of energy by means of *windmills*. Windmills are tall structures which harness the power of the wind to do work. For instance, they are used for grinding (and storing) grain. They are also used as pumps.

Holland's most important products are dairy products. The Dutch export their cheeses to countries all over the world. They also raise the best milk-producing breed of cattle in the world, the Holstein-Friesian. Because of the rich soil there, Holland also produces beautiful tulip, hyacinth, and other flower bulbs.

The Dutch eat primarily potatoes, cheeses, stews and meats. They also like french-fried potatoes called *chips*. Their main meal is dinner, which is a time when most families sit down and eat together.

Traditionally, the Dutch have used blue Delft tiles to add decorative touches to their homes, which is evident in paintings by Vermeer, Pieter de Hooch, and other Dutch artists. The Rijks Museum in Amsterdam is home to "Night Watch," a famous painting by Rembrandt.

The Dutch wear wooden shoes, called *klompen,* to protect their feet from the damp ground. Today, people all over the world wear similar shoes called *clogs,* which are derived from the Dutch klompen.

Ice skating, soccer, swimming and baseball are the most popular sports in Holland. The children of Holland play many games that are similar to American games, such as leap frog, jumping rope and hide and seek.

A great replica of Holland in miniature has been constructed in a Dutch town called Madurodam. The replica stretches over an acre of land and contains life-like reproductions of different cities in Holland. The miniature towns are complete with ferry boats and buses which really work. The miniatures at Madurodam are a popular source of entertainment in Holland.

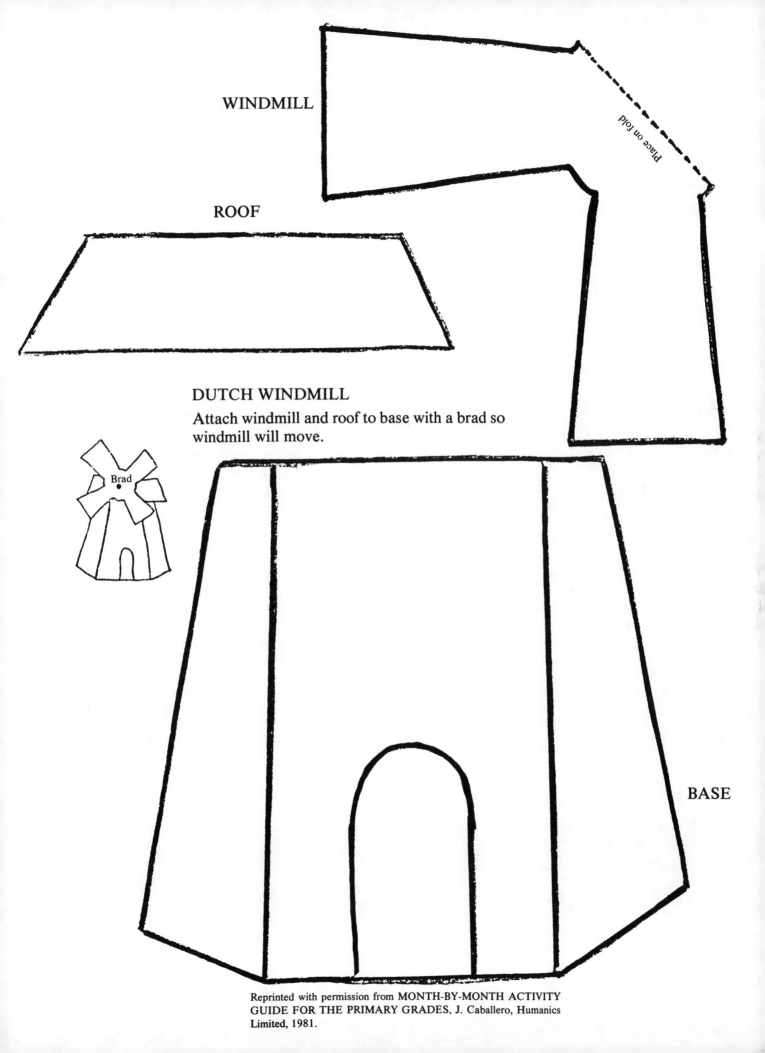

WINDMILL

Place on fold

ROOF

DUTCH WINDMILL

Attach windmill and roof to base with a brad so
windmill will move.

Brad

BASE

Reprinted with permission from MONTH-BY-MONTH ACTIVITY
GUIDE FOR THE PRIMARY GRADES, J. Caballero, Humanics
Limited, 1981.

I AM A PRETTY LITTLE DUTCH GIRL
(traditional)

1. *I am a pretty little Dutch girl.*
   As pretty as pretty can be, be, be.
   And all the boys in my hometown
   Are crazy over me, me, me.

2. *My mother wanted peaches,*
   My mother wanted pears,
   My mother wanted fifty cents
   To mend the broken stairs

3. *My boyfriend gave me peaches*
   My boyfriend gave me pears
   My boyfriend gave me fifty cents
   And kissed me on the stairs.

4. *My mother ate the peaches,*
   My brother ate the pears,
   My father ate the fifty cents
   And fell right down the stairs.

5. *My mother called the doctor,*
   My brother called the nurse,
   But all my father really did
   Was stay in bed at Gravenhurst.

Since Holland's chief industries depend heavily on the sea, many of the Dutch children's games are related to the sea. Water activities such as swimming, rowing, sailing and fishing are very popular with the Dutch, along with team sports, such as basketball and soccer. Bowling on the grass is another favorite game. Other Dutch games and toys which are familiar to us in the United States are: balls, hoops, marbles, tops, hop-scotch, kite flying, leap frog, rope jumping and tag. The most popular sport in Holland, however, is ice skating. Some skaters carry little sails to catch the wind and help move them quickly over the ice. When the canals freeze over for the first time each winter, the schools declare a holiday and everyone goes skating.

The following Dutch games are played the same way as the American games:

Leap Frog—*Haasje Over*
Jump Rope—*Touwtje*
Hop Scotch—*Hinkelen*
Hide and Seek—*Verstoppertje*
Tag—*Krifgergfe*
Yoyo—*Jojo*

RECILPES

Dutch food is rich and filling. The people like thick soups, such as the *erwtensoep*. Seafood, chiefly herring, makes up a major part of the Dutch diet. Smoked eel and Zealand oysters are Dutch specialties. Edam and Gouda cheeses from Holland are world famous.

Chocolate Bread

Bread
Butter
Chocolate Chips

Spread bread with butter and sprinkle chocolate chips on top. Heat if you like.

Stamppot

Potatoes
Cabbage
Mixed vegetables
Meat (chuck roast or round steak)
Salt, pepper, garlic

Cube all ingredients and place in a large pot. Cook slowly on low heat until tender, about 2 hours. Add water as necessary.

Erwent Soup (Pea Soup)

1 can condensed pea soup
1 can condensed beef consomme
½ soup can milk

Mix all ingredients and heat until the mixture begins to boil. Serves four.

VOCABULARY

one—*een*
two—*twee*
three—*drie*
four—*vier*
five—*vijf*
six—*zes*
seven—*seven*
eight—*acht*
nine—*negen*
ten—*tien*
hello—*hello*
goodbye—*tot ziens*
peace—*vrede*
goodnight—*goede nacht*
happy—*blij*
I—*ik*
love—*houvan*
you—*jou*

GERMANY

Color the German flag.

Can you name these places?

1. _____ .

2. _____ .

3. _____ .

Answers: Rhine River, Hamburg, Berlin

black

red

gold

135

WEST GERMANY

Germany, located in Central Europe, is divided into two countries. The Federal Republic of Germany, or West Germany, has a parliamentary form of government. The German Democratic Republic, or East Germany, is a communist country.

Before World War II, Germany was a single country. World War II began when Adolf Hitler, leader of Germany and founder of the Nazi party, launched a German takeover of Austria, Czechoslovakia and Poland. On September 3, 1939, Great Britian and France declared war on Germany to help defend Poland. Germany had formed an alliance with Italy and Japan, and these nations were known as the Axis Powers. The United States declared war on the Axis Powers when Japan bombed Pearl Harbor, in Hawaii, in December of 1941. Germany surrendered on May 3, 1945, and when Japan surrendered in August of 1945, World War II was over.

After the war ended, the Allied Powers (Great Britain, France, the United States, and Russia) divided Germany into four military zines. Each Allied Power occupied one zone. The alliance between Russia and the other three countries soon collapsed, however, and England, France, and the United States decided to unite their three zones. These three zones were combined to become the country West Germany. The Russian zone became East Germany and was a Russian satellite country. Until late 1989, individual freedom in East Germany was sharply curtailed and communication or travel between East Germany and West Germany or other free nations was virtually prohibited by East Germany's communist government. Now East Germany and West Germany have decided to join and become one Germany again.

Manufacturing is Germany's strongest industry and has been in fact an important factor in its rapid economic recovery after World War II. Today, Germany's total production ranks fourth in the world after the United States, the U.S.S.R. and Japan. Germany's main industries include iron, steel, scientific instruments, textiles and chemicals.

Since West Germany's soil is poor, much of the nation's food must be imported. The Rhine and Moselle River valleys are the source of fine wines.

West Germany has a public education system in which children attend elementary schools for eight or nine years. In the fourth or fifth grade children take a test to determine whether or not they will attend high school, which is designed to prepare them for college. If the children do not score high enough on the test, they will go to vocational school instead of high school when they finish elementary school.

DRAW A GERMAN CASTLE

There are many castles in Germany, especially along the Rhine River. Some of them are very well kept and can be rented for weddings or for "holiday" (European vacation). They can be very large, such as the one pictured below. Draw your own German castle.

Photo by C.T. Caballero.

German castle on the Rhine River.

VOCABULARY

English words borrowed from German

hamburger
delicatessen
pretzel
sauerkraut
kindergarten

RECIPES

Wiener Schnitzel

veal cutlets
salt
flour, eggs, bread crumbs (quantity depends on how many cutlets you are fixing)

Dip the cutlets into beaten eggs, then flour and bread crumbs. Fry in hot oil until golden brown.

German Farmer's Breakfast
Bauernfrühstuck

6 bacon slices
1 green pepper, sliced
2 T. onion, chopped
3 boiled potatoes, peeled and cubed
½ C. grated cheese
6 eggs

Fry bacon and drain off all but 3 T. oil. Add vegetables and seasonings. Cook about 5 minutes until potatoes are brown. Sprinkle cheese over contents and stir. Break eggs into pan over vegetables and cook until eggs are done.

The Germans eat a lot of sauerkraut and sausages. Pretzels are also popular and are often served with mustard.

Some of the sausages served in Germany with German potato salad and sauerkraut are:

Bratwurst, made of pork and veal with tangy flavor

Bauernwurst, a farmer's sausage with a coarse texture, containing mustard seeds

Knockwurst, smoked-cooked beef sausage similar to frankfurters

Frankfurter, mild seasoned pork and beef sausage, with no extenders

Currywurst, chargrilled veal sausage with curry sauce

Munich Weisswurst, a pork and veal sausage made with mild spices and parsley

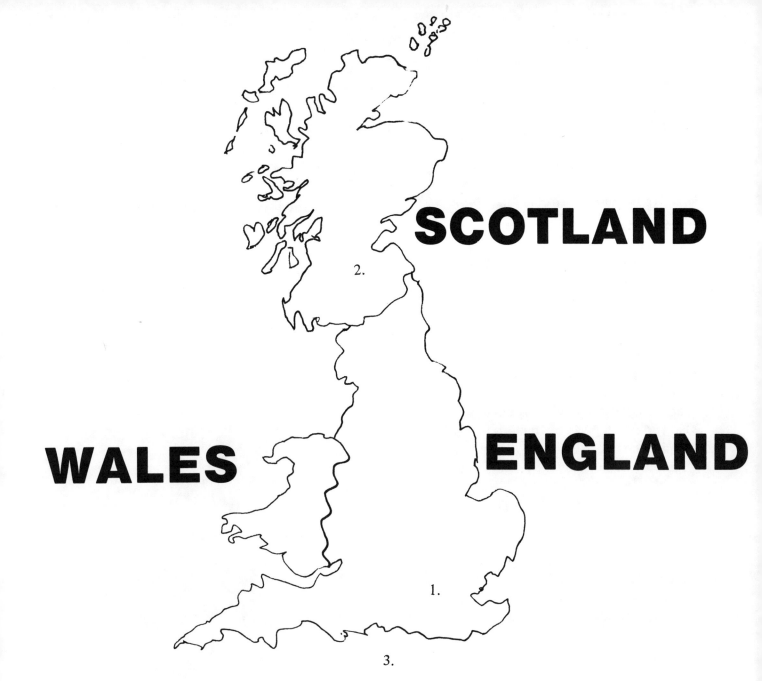

SCOTLAND

WALES

ENGLAND

2.

1.

3.

Can you name these places?

1. _____.

2. _____.

3. _____.

Answers: London, Edinburgh, English Channel

Color the flag of the United Kingdom.

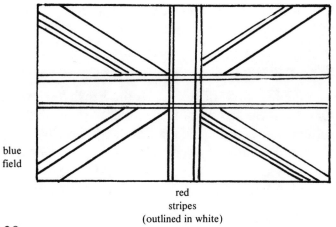

blue field

red stripes (outlined in white)

SCOTLAND, ENGLAND, WALES

Scotland, England, Wales and Northern Ireland make up the United Kingdom of Great Britain. Thus the United Kingdom is spread over two islands: the island of Great Britain which contains England, Scotland and Wales, and the island of Ireland, which contains Northern Ireland and the Republic of Ireland.

English is the official language throughout Great Britain. In different parts of the United Kingdom, however, English can be spoken very differently. For instance, the people of Scotland have a distinct accent and pronounce the letter "R" with a trill of the tongue. In addition, in certain parts of the United Kingdom people speak ancient dialects. For example, some people in a part of Scotland known as the Highlands speak Gaelic, an ancient Celtic language. Gaelic is also spoken in parts of Ireland. In Wales, some people who live in isolated villages speak Welsh, which is another ancient Celtic language.

SCOTLAND

Scotland, about the size of South Carolina, has three main land regions: the Highlands, the Central Lowlands and the Southern Uplands. The majority of the people in Scotland live in the Central Lowlands, where the best farmland and mineral resources are found.

The River Clyde is Scotland's most important river. There are many lakes, called lochs, in the Highland valleys. One of these, Loch Ness, is famous for its "monster." Many people claim to have seen a creature thirty feet long in this lake.

The capital of Scotland is Edinburgh. The four major cities of Scotland are Edinburgh, Glasgow, Aberdeen and Dundee. Many people leave Scotland each year because of limited job opportunities.

The Church of Scotland, the Presbyterian Church, is Scotland's official church. Many other religions are practiced in Scotland, however. Scotland's school system is separate from England's, Wales' or Northern Ireland's. Most children attend public schools from the time they're five years old until they're sixteen. Scotland has eight universities.

Many Scotish traditions began with the *clans*, large families with common ancestors, such as the MacDonalds or the MacGregors. Some of the favorite foods of Scottish people are herring, mutton stew, roast beef and lamb.

In the Highlands, there are many vast estates belonging to *lairds* (land owners). A few Highlanders wear *kilts*, which look like plaid skirts, instead of trousers. Most wear tweed suits and woolen sweaters, however, produced in Scotland's woolen mills. The bagpipes, a complicated wind instrument, and bagpipe music are another Highland tradition. The bagpipe and the kilt have become symbols of Scotland (see photo).

The doll is dressed in a kilt and is carrying a bagpipe.

ENGLAND

England is located in the southeastern part of the island of Great Britian. It was colonized by Celts 3,000 years ago, ruled by Romans for nearly 400 years, and then conquered by peoples known as Saxons and Angles. It became known as Angle-land (which evolved into England) after the Angles, and the people spoke a language called Anglo-Saxon.

Prior to 1066, the English were already writing government documents, chronicles and laws in their native language—an accomplishment unsurpassed in western Europe. In 1066, Normans conquered England in what is known as the Norman Conquest. After the conquest, the Anglo-Saxon dialect merged with French, the language of the Norman conquerors, which greatly enriched and expanded the native tongue with new words and concepts. Later Vikings, Scandinavians from Norway and Denmark and French Huguenots settled in England, each bringing further contributions to the English language. This assimilation of many races in England resulted in the development of a unique language. It is the language in which the poetry and prose of Chaucer, Shakespeare, Wordsworth, Keats, Bacon and Macaulay are written and, with relatively little change, the language we in the United States speak today.

The land in England is rich and is used primarily for agriculture. Approximately one third of this land is used for the cultivation of crops and approximately two thirds is used for pasture and grazing. Nine percent of the country is covered with forests.

From the time they are five years old until they are sixteen, children in England are required to attend school full time. Many children aged three to five attend nursery schools. Additional educational opportunities are available at England's universities, polytechnics, vocational schools and schools that offer parttime courses.

WALES

A great deal of the Welsh countryside is made up of moors and mountains. As noted previously, some villages are very isolated.

The Welsh people are famous for their choirs and music festivals, and for their poetry and writing competitions which attract visitors from many countries. Wales also has many rugby football teams. Rugby football is a little like American football and is very popular in Wales.

GAMES IN THE UNITED KINGDOM

CHARLIE OVER THE WATER

Twenty or more players form a circle. "Charlie" stands in the center facing two players who hold a stick 12 inches above and parallel to the ground to represent a bridge. The circle players join hands and skip around singing:

Charlie over the water
Charlie over the sea
Charlie catch a blackbird
Can't catch me.

As the last line is said, Charlie jumps over the stick and runs to tag the circle players before they stoop. If he is successful, the tagged player becomes Charlie; if not, he must be Charlie again.

The game goes back to the exile of Charles II of England in France. He was urged by the Scots to come back over the water.

SCOTS AND ENGLISH
(Stealing Sticks)

This game calls for twenty or more players. The playing area, a large field, is marked into two equal parts. Six sticks are placed in a small goal at the end of each part. The players are divided into two equal groups and take their places, one team in each part of the field. The players are to touch their opponents' goal without being tagged and bring one stick at a time back to their own goal. No player may be tagged if he has secured a stick and is returning to his goal. If he is tagged while in the opponents' territory before reaching the goal, he becomes a prisoner until one of his team comes and touches him. If a team has lost any of its members to the other side as prisoners, that team cannot retrieve any more sticks until all the prisoners are "freed." Whichever team retrieves all its sticks first, wins.

From GAMES AND SPORTS THE WORLD AROUND Sarah Ethridegehunt, New York: The Ronald Press Co.

RECIPES

Sugar Crisps*

½ stick butter
¼ C. sugar
½ C. flour
drop of vanilla
2 t. milk

Mix the butter and sugar together. Slowly add the flour. Add the vanilla and part of the milk. (Add more milk, if it seems too dry.) Place the mixture in balls on an ungreased cookie sheet and bake in a 350 degree oven for 10 minutes.

Serve crisps with hot tea. The British are known for teatime. You can do as they do and have your teatime, too.

Yorkshire Pudding**

2 eggs
1 C. flour
1 C. milk
3 T. oil
dash of salt

Beat eggs and gradually add flour and milk, alternating. Add salt. Refrigerate for two or more hours. Heat oil in 425 degree oven in a 10 inch pie pan. Remove from oven and stir batter into the hot dish. Cook in oven for about 30 minutes, until the pudding has risen and browned. Serve with beef.

English Tea Scones

2 C. flour
6 T. butter

Mix flour and butter with hands. Then add:

3 T. sugar
½ C. raisins
2 beaten eggs

Mix with hands lightly and add ⅓ C. milk. Make sure the dough isn't too sticky. Place half the dough on a floured surface and pat in a circle ½ inch thick. Cut into sections with spatula and bake 10 minutes at 400 degrees.

Scottish Shortbread

1 C. butter
2 C. flour
½ C. sifted confectioners' sugar
dash salt

Cream butter. Sift together dry ingredients. Blend into butter and pat into an ungreased 9x9 inch pan. Pierce with a fork every ½ inch. Bake at 325 degrees for 30 minutes. Cut into squares and serve.

VOCABULARY

American	English
candy	sweet
apartment	flat
elevator	lift
first floor	ground floor
second floor	first floor
vest	waistcoat
policeman	bobby
sidewalk	pavement
shopping bag	carrier bag
car trunk	boot
car hood	bonnet
underpass	subway
subway	underground
truck	lorry
garbage collector	dustman

143

Scotland

IRELAND

1.

3.

2.

Wales

England

Can you name these places?

1. _____ .
2. _____ .
3. _____ .

Answers: Northern Ireland, Ireland, Dublin

Color the Irish flag.

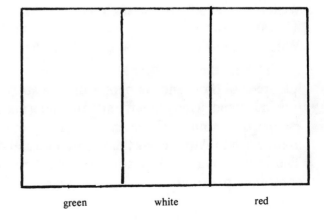

green   white   red

145

IRELAND

The Emerald Isle received its nickname because of its brilliant emerald green and olive green fields. They are particularly brilliant when seen from the air. Each field in Ireland is surrounded by a hedge or stone wall. Since lumber is scarce, you seldom see wood fences in Ireland. The countryside is full of castles and stone cottages with thatched roofs. Ireland is a land full of myths and magic and tales of "little people."

The Celtic Gaels are the ancestors of the Irish people and Ireland acquired its language from the Celts. They were fierce warriors. They were also historians and worshippers of nature. The Celtic children were taught songs and stories and passed them on to the next generation. The custom of hanging mistletoe at Christmas can be traced back to the Celts.

Christianity came to Ireland in 432 A.D. when St. Patrick, a Briton, brought the religion to the isle. During his lifetime he converted much of Ireland to the Catholic faith. He also preserved the Celt's customs, however, unless they were in direct conflict with the Catholic religion. Our Halloween is believed to be a result of the merger of the gaelic harvest festival and the Christian feast of All Saints.

Ireland has a history of great writers. Some of Ireland's best known writers are Jonathan Swift who wrote *Gulliver's Travels;* George Bernard Shaw, who won a Nobel Prize for literature and wrote the play *Pygmalion;* Oscar Wilde who wrote *The Picture of Dorian Gray;* and the poet William Butler Yeats, who also won the Nobel Prize. Ireland has some of the world's greatest writers in recent times, such as James Joyce. The ancestors of John F. Kennedy, Woodrow Wilson, and Eugene O'Neill came from Ireland.

During the Great Potato Famine of 1945, hundreds of thousands of people died of starvation in Ireland. Many others sailed to America to escape the famine. For awhile, there were as many Irish in America as there were in Ireland. The Irish brought their traditions with them to contribute to America's varied heritage.

The Republic of Ireland is a land of warm hearted people who welcome the tourist. The Republic of Ireland is indeed delightful to visit. There are wonderful lakes, streams, and castles to explore. You can kiss the Blarney Stone for luck, and enjoy a medieval dinner at Bunratty Castle.

Northern Ireland, a part of the United Kingdom, has soft green scenery. The coast roads to the Glens of Antrim, County Down and the Giants Causeway take you past lovely sights and countryside. Unfortunately, the unrest between the Catholics and Protestants in Northern Ireland has been in the news almost daily. We must watch the situation to see the future of this country.

St. Patrick's Day celebrates the anniversary of St. Patrick's death on March 17, 461. At the age of 16, he was captured by pirates and sold into slavery. Six years later, he escaped and began preparing for his religious life. He became a priest and then a bishop. He was sent to the Emerald Isle in 432. This patron saint of Ireland spent his life trying to free the Irish from Paganism. He established 365 churches and schools, a college, consecrated two bishops and Christianized most of the population.

RECIPES

Irish Stew

2 lbs. lamb, cut into chunks
2 T. flour
dash salt, pepper, garlic, sugar
2 T. oil
2 onions, chopped
6-8 chopped carrots
4-6 chopped potatoes

Roll lamb in flour, salt and pepper. Fry in hot oil. Add garlic and onion. Add water and sugar and simmer about one hour. Add carrots, potatoes, and more onions (if desired). Cook until vegetables are tender.

Irish Candy*

2 egg whites
1 t. vanilla
¾ C. granulated sugar
1 pkg. (6 oz.) chocolate bits
¼ C. nuts (optional)
⅛ t. cream of tartar
⅛ t. salt

Beat egg white, salt, cream of tartar and vanilla until peaks form. Gradually add sugar and beat until stiff. Fold in chocolate and nuts. Drop onto cookie sheets. Bake at 300 degrees for 25 minutes.

VOCABULARY

While many people in Ireland speak English, some people use the old Celtic language called ERSE.

father—*athair*
great—*mar*
singer—*baird*
I am going—*taim ag dul*
he gives—*do beir*

Other Celtic languages include:
Breton (France)
Cornish (England)
Manx (Isle of Man)
Gaelic (Scotland)
Welsh (Wales)

COCKLES AND MUSSELS

1. *In Dublin's fair city, Where girls are so pretty,*
   I first set my eyes on sweet Molly Malone,
   As she wheeled her wheelbarrow,
   Through streets broad and narrow,
   Crying cockles and mussels, alive, alive, oh!

CHORUS
   Alive, alive oh! Alive, alive oh!
   Crying cockles and mussels alive, alive oh!

2. *She was a fish monger and sure 'twas no wonder*
   Since so were her father and mother before;
   They each wheeled a barrow
   Through streets broad and narrow,
   Crying cockles and mussels, alive, alive oh!

3. *She died of a fever, and no one could save her,*
   And that was the end of dear Molly Malone.
   But her ghost wheels the barrow
   Through street broad and narrow,
   Crying cockles and mussels, alive, alive oh!

NORWAY

FINLAND

SWEDEN

DENMARK

1.

2.

3.

4.

Can you name these places?

1. _____.

2. _____.

3. _____.

4. _____.

SCANDINAVIA

DENMARK

Denmark, Norway, and Sweden make up the Scandinavian countries. Denmark consists of a peninsula and 482 nearby islands. One of Denmark's provinces, however, lies off the northeastern coast of Canada, 1,300 miles away. The peninsula, Jutland, shares a 42 mile border with West Germany.

Copenhagen is Denmark's capital and its largest city. Over a fourth of the Danes live in the Copenhagen area and almost half the country's industries are there. The famous Tivoli Gardens, an amusement center, is in Copenhagen. Other interesting sights are old Copenhagen, Central Station, the Town Hall Square and the giant country-style nightclub and dancehall where over 300 Danes gather nightly to eat, dance and see a floor show.

The land in Denmark is poor in natural resources. Denmark must sell products to other countries to pay for the fuels and metals that it must import. Nonetheless the people of Denmark are prosperous and have one of the world's highest standards of living. Denmark is famous for its butter, cheeses, bacon, ham, and other processed foods. It is also known for its manufactured goods, including furniture and silverware. Denmark is also a great shipping and fishing nation.

The government is a constitutional monarchy with a king or queen, a prime minister, and a parliament. Government is divided into three branches—executive, legislative, and judicial. The monarch has little actual power.

Most Danes eat four meals a day—breakfast, lunch, dinner and a late-evening supper. Dinner is the only hot meal of the day.

Almost all of the people in Denmark belong to the Evangelical Lutheran Church. They have freedom to worship as they please.

SWEDEN

Sweden is a country of lowlands and mountains in the eastern part of the Scandinavian Peninsula. It has one of the highest standards of living in the world and on the average its people enjoy the longest life expectancy of the citizens of any country in the world. Its government is a constitutional monarchy. It has one of the most extensive social welfare programs in the world, all paid for with taxes.

The predominant religion in Sweden is Evangelical Lutheran. The official language is Swedish. English, German, Finnish, Norwegian and Danish are also spoken.

The cold winter in the north lasts more than seven months. You can see the midnight sun in Lapland, the northernmost province of Norrland. For six weeks in mid-summer the sun never sets. Reindeer-herding nomads still follow their ancestors' way of life in Lapland.

Stockholm, Sweden, is surrounded by forests. It spreads over fourteen separate islands, each connected by bridges. Lake Malaren, which extends into the city, is often covered with beautiful sailboats. Stockholm has many restaurants, theaters, and museums. Some of the museums are unique open air museums. The mysterious flagship Wasa is also located here.

NORWAY

Oslo, Norway depends heavily on the sea. The Kon-Tiki Raft of Thor Heyerdahl and the polar ship, Fram, in which the Norwegian explorer Nansen went to the North Pole, are located here. The Oslo Fjord, sixty miles long, contains the Tryvanns Tower, from which you may see the entire fjord.

FINLAND

The capital of Finland is Helsinki. Finland is a beautiful country of lakes and forests. Like other Scandinavian countries, it is famous for products made of wood, including furniture, houses, and boats. Many Finnish people work in the fishing industry.

FINLAND

SWEDEN

NORWAY

DENMARK

151

Color the flags of the Scandinavian countries.

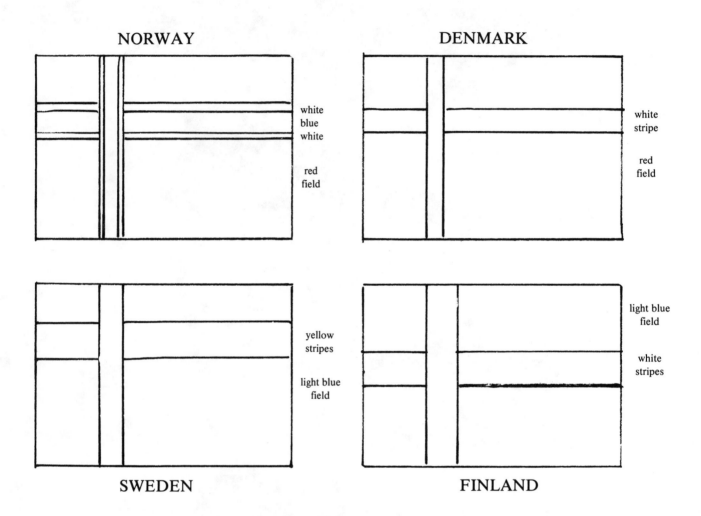

NORWAY

white
blue
white

red
field

DENMARK

white
stripe

red
field

SWEDEN

yellow
stripes

light blue
field

FINLAND

light blue
field

white
stripes

Use marshmallows, macaroni (colored with food coloring), colored cellophane and any other interesting materials to create Scandinavian flags.

RECIPES

Swedish Meatballs

1 lb. ground beef
1 onion, minced
garlic, salt, pepper
1 beaten egg
crushed corn flakes or cracker crumbs

Mix all ingredients together. Shape into balls and cook slowly in a sauce made of lemon juice and 1 jar of grape jelly.

Norwegian Flarn*

1 T. flour
½ C. sugar
½ C. butter
2 T. milk
⅔ C. blanched almonds

Mix ingredients in skillet and stir over low heat until butter melts. Drop spoonfuls onto cookie sheet and bake in 375 degree oven until brown.

Finnish Shakes

Fresh strawberries, raspberries or blueberries
Cold milk
1 T. sugar

Wash the berries and cut off the stems. Cut into pieces and put into blender. Add milk and sugar. Mix until blended.

Danish Krumkakes

2 eggs
⅔ C. sugar
½ C. butter
1¾ C. flour
1 t. vanilla

Combine ingredients to form dough. Cook 1 tablespoon of dough about 2 minutes on each side in a small amount of butter. As soon as you remove it, roll it on a wooden spoon handle. These wafers may be filled with ice cream or jelly.

VOCABULARY

Swedish, Danish and Norwegian languages are similar to each other. People from Sweden, Denmark and Norway can understand each others' language. Many Finnish people also speak Swedish.

SWEDISH

man—*mannen*
you—*du*
house—*huse*

DANISH

man—*manden*
oxygen—*ilt*

NORWEGIAN

Norwegian folk tales—*Norske folkeeuentyr*
History of the Norwegian people—*Det norske folks historie*

Finnish Troll

153

GREECE

Can you name these places?

1. _____.
2. _____.
3. _____.

Color the Greek flag.

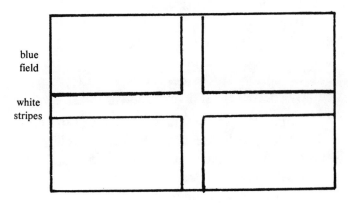

blue
field

white
stripes

155

GREECE

Greece is a small country in southern Europe. There are approximately 10,244,000 people in the entire country. The Ionian Islands, the large island of Crete, and most of the Aegean Islands are part of Greece. A total of 437 islands make up 27% of the country.

Greece is the least industrialized and most rural of all European countries. Approximately half of the Greek people earn a living by agriculture. Much of the land is mountainous and unfertile, however, and many people in Greece are poor. Many still ride donkeys because cars and gasoline are very expensive in Greece.

In ancient times, Greece represented the epitome of human civilization and achievement. In fact ancient Greece can be called the birthplace of modern western civilization. Much of our knowledge and practice in art, mathematics, astronomy and philosophy are based on work done by the ancient Greeks. Pythagoras and Euclid were two famous mathematicians from ancient Greece. Euclid is called the father of geometry. Socrates, Plato and Aristotle were famous philosophers. Ptolemy was a famous astronomer, and Phidias was a famous architect. The contributions made by all of these men are still studied and used today.

In addition, we owe our form of government to the ancient Greeks. Ancient Greece was the first *democracy*. Many of Greece's modern governments, however, have been undemocratic. Unfortunately, many of them have also been unstable.

The original Olympic Games were held in ancient Greece. The name "Olympic" comes from the ancient Greek religion. The ancient Greeks believed in many gods, ruled by Zeus who was the most powerful, who lived together on Mt. Olympus. The first Olympic Games were held to honor the Greek gods. Sports, particularly soccer, are still very popular in Greece.

Today the predominant religion in Greece is the Greek Orthodox Church. The church is a very powerful and important force in Greek society and most of the Greek people are members. In fact, Greeks must be members of the church before they can obtain official papers to advance in Greek society. Greek Orthodox Church Festivals are also very important to the Greek people. Often people wear colorful national costumes as part of the celebration. The festivals often include folk dancing. Two of the dances are called the *Calamatiano* and the *Sirtako*.

Tourism is an important part of the national economy in Greece. Athens, the capital of Greece, is one of the world's most historic cities. Ninety-five percent of Greece's tourists come to Athens. Many come to see the Acropolis, a hill which was the center of ancient Athens. Today the ruins of the Parthenon, a temple dedicated to the goddess Athena, and other ancient temples still stand there.

Greek food consists primarily of lamb and seafood. Greek dishes often contain olive oil, fresh tomatoes and lemon. Most Greeks have nothing but coffee for breakfast, but they take a long time over lunch which is a large meal and very filling. Afterwards, they may take a nap. The evening meal is late and may last a long time also.

Greek families are very close. The Greeks raise their children in a very strict manner. Public education in Greece is free and primary education is compulsory. Students wear blue and white uniforms in the state schools.

ART ACTIVITY

Try to draw the three architectural orders.

Doric (6th century B.C.) Heavy wooden beams.

Ionic (5th century B.C.) Scroll decorations added to the capital and delicate fluting added to the column.

Corinthian (4th century B.C.) Elaborate decoration added to the capital. Columns became more slender.

Pebble Chase

4-10 players

Materials: pebbles or marbles

Before starting, players choose a "safe" place some distance from the playing area. Players form a line standing side by side, facing the leader. Players extend their hands with palms pressed together.

The leader takes the pebble and presses it between his palms. He slowly passes down the line and pretends to drop the pebble into each player's hands. When he does in fact drop the pebble in a player's hands, that player then runs to the safe spot and then back to the leader. The other players chase him and if he gets caught before returning to the leader, he must let the person who caught him be the leader. If he returns safely, he becomes the leader.

Odd or Even

2 or more players— if more than 2, pair off

Materials: ten beans for each player

One player puts an amount of beans in his hands and extends them to his opponent. He asks if the amount is odd or even. If the opponent is incorrect, he must give one bean to the player. If the opponent is correct, the player gives him one bean. The process continues until one player has no more beans.

RECICIPES

Some popular Greek Foods:

Moussaka—layers of eggplant and ground beef
Feta cheese—made from sheep or goat milk
Ouzo—a licorice flavored wine
Baklava—honey and almond pastry
Retsina—white wine
Soupa avgolemono—lemon flavored chicken soup
Dolmades—stuffed grape leaves
Olives

Crema Karamela

1¾ C. sugar
5 eggs
1 qt. warmed milk
1 t. vanilla
1½ qt. mold or 12 custard cups

Melt 1 cup sugar over medium heat, stirring constantly until caramel consistency. Pour into bottom of mold or custard cups. Warm milk. Beat eggs with ¾ cup sugar. Add milk gradually to eggs. Add vanilla. Pour into mold or cups and place in a pan of hot water. Then bake at 350 degrees until firm. Cool at room temperature and place in refrigerator until ready to serve.

GREEK ALPHABET

alpha
beta
gamma
delta
epsilon
zeta
eta
theta
iota
kappa
lambda
mu
nu
xi
omicron
pi
rho
sigma
tau
upsilon
phi
chi
psi
omega

VOCABULARY

one—*en*
two—*dio*
three—*tria*
four—*tessara*
five—*pente*
six—*x*
seven—*efta*
eight—*okto*
nine—*ennea*
ten—*deka*

English words borrowed from the Greeks

monarch	*physical*
architect	*pharmacy*
character	*syllable*
rhyme	*synonym*
rhythm	*antonym*
rheumatism	*homonym*
alphabet	*pseudonym*
apostrophe	*ptomaine*
atmosphere	*pneumonia*
cellophane	*xylophone*

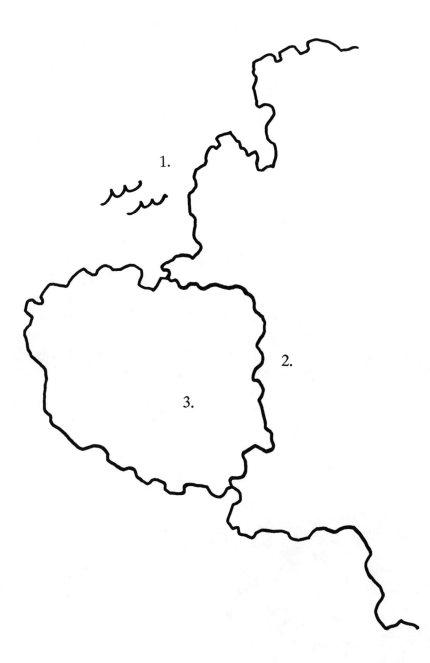

1.

2.

3.

POLAND

Color the Polish flag.

Can you name these places?

1. _____ .

2. _____ .

3. _____ .

white

red

POLAND

Poland is bounded by Czechoslovakia, Russia, Germany and the Baltic Sea. Poland means *country of the plain.* Poland has many canals which make shipment of coal and machinery and other goods easy and inexpensive. Poland relies on its canals and rivers to help with the exporting and importing of goods. Poland also has rich, fertile soil which allows the country to produce large quantities of grain and vegetables.

Warsaw is the capital of Poland.

Poles have endured repeated invasion and foreign domination of their country during the past 200 years. Poland has been under Communist rule since 1946. Jews and Germans made up much of the population prior to the Nazi invasion of World War II. Since then, Poland has become a country inhabited almost entirely by non-Jewish Poles. Most of the minority groups were transported to their country of origin after the war. Many Polish Jews migrated to Israel.

Most of the people in Poland are Roman Catholic, although the Communists discourage religion. Education is free to all children through the age of fourteen. Classes are taught in the Polish language until the fifth grade and then they must be taught in Russian.

Some famous Poles are: Frederic Chopin, the composer; Marie Curie, the famous scientist who discovered radium; Copernicus, the astronomer; and Kazimierz Funk, the discoverer of the vitamin.

Soccer is the most popular sport and form of recreation in Poland. Polish foods are rich and full of tradition. There are definite Russian, German and Jewish influences on the cuisine, but it has a flavor all its own. Some Polish foods include Polish sausage, Chrusciki, Mizeria ze Smietana (cucumbers in sour cream), and Zupa Jablkowa (apple soup).

160

POLISH LULLABY

This is a popular Polish lullaby that is sung in a chant with no music.

Ahh, Ahh
Kotki dwa
Czarny bude obid dwa
Nic nie bede az robili
Tylko (Steven, or name of child)z bawili.

Ah, Ah
Two kittens
One is black, the other tan
With nothing else to do
But play with Steven.

The paper cutouts of Poland (pictured) are an example of their folk art. Note the fine details. Create your own paper cutout.

RECIPES

Polish sausage or *kielbasa* can be purchased at most stores.

Chrusciki
4 egg yolks
1 T. vinegar
1 T. sugar
dash of salt
1 C. flour
Combine all ingredients. Knead dough and roll it out. Cut into strips 1" x 3", then slit in the middle of each strip. Pull one end of the strip through the slit. Deep fry until lightly browned. Top with powdered sugar.

Mizeria ze Smietana
(Cucumbers in sour cream)
3 C. sliced cucumbers
1 C. sour cream
dash of salt
2 T. dill weed or chopped dill
Sprinkle cucumbers with salt and let stand a few minutes. Pat dry. Stir dill and cucumbers into sour cream and serve.

Zupa Jablkowa
(Apple soup)
6-7 apples
pot of water
¾ C. sugar
dash cinnamon
½ C. lemon juice
1 C. whipping cream
Peel and core apples and cook in water until soft. Put into blender and blend into applesauce. Mix in sugar and cinnamon. Chill. Just before serving, mix cream into mixture. If desired, shred one apple, soak it in lemon juice and add it to the mixture.
One 16 oz. jar of applesauce and 1 cup water may be substituted for fresh apples.

Mushrooms in Sour Cream
fresh mushrooms
1 T. butter
1 t. flour
sour cream
salt, pepper, dill or parsley
Cook mushrooms in butter a couple of minutes. Stir in flour and cook a minute longer. Stir in sour cream and seasonings. Serve warm.

VOCABULARY
one—*jeden (YEH-den)*
two—*dwa (dvah)*
three—*trzy (tshih)*
four—*cztery (CHTEH-rih)*
five—*piec (pyehn-ch)*
six—*szesc (shensh-ch)*
seven—*siedem (SHEH-dem)*
eight—*osiem (OH-shehm)*
nine—*dziewiec (DZHEH-vehnch)*
ten—*dziesiec (DZHEH-shench)*

How are you?—*Jak sie masz?*
goodnight—*dobranoc*
good day—*dowidzenia*
I like you. —*Ja cie lubie.*
What is your name?—*Jak sie nazywasz?*
What do you want to eat?—*Co chcesz jesc?*

RUSSIA

2.

1.

3.

Color the flag of the U.S.S.R.

Can you name these places?

1. _____.

2. _____.

3. _____.

yellow

red

Answers: Moscow, Leningrad, U.S.S.R.

163

RUSSIA

Russia is the common name for the Union of Soviet Socialist Republics. Moscow (*Moskva* in Russian) became the capital of the Soviet Union on March 13, 1918. In the center of the city are located the Kremlin and Red Square, which constitute the political center of the nation. Lenin was the father of the modern Russian political system and is revered as a hero by the Russian people. Lenin's tomb is located in Red Square. Millions of pilgrims (visitors) visit his tomb each year. St. Basil's Cathedral is also situated in Red Square. It is perhaps the most recognizable symbol of Russia. (See page 166.) This beautiful cathedral was built in the sixteenth century.

In 1985, Mikhail S. Gorbachev came into power as the head of the Communist Party. The Russian word "perestroika" refers to the economic and political reform proposed by Gorbachev. Under this reform, non-Communist social organizations can be formed, with permission from the government. Another Russian term that has become known worldwide is "glasnost," a policy of Gorbachev's that allows more freedom of expression than in the past.

Another important city in Russia is Leningrad, formerly called St. Petersburg. It was renamed in honor of Lenin. Leningrad was once the home of the Russian czars (rulers) and has many beautiful palaces, gardens, and scenic canals similar to those you find in Venice, Italy.

Russians value a variety of cultural activities, such as the circus, opera, and ballet. There are many circus companies that travel throughout Russia. These companies include fantastic acts such as trapeze, acrobats, balancing teams, jugglers, and animals. Russian children enjoy seeing the well-trained black bears actually play ice hockey! The ballet is also a very popular art form that is enjoyed by everyone and Russian ballet companies are among the finest in the world.

Russian winters last more than half the year, with temperatures often dropping below zero. A highlight of the winter season is the winter festival, much like our winter holiday season. Father Frost and the Snow Maiden greet the children and give them gifts. *Snovan Ghodham* is the Russian greeting "Happy New Year!"

Russian Dolls

Matrioska Dolls—Symbol of happiness and good luck for the New Year.

Father Frost is the Russian equivalent to America's Santa Claus. He greets the children with *Snovan Ghodham* (Happy New Year). You can make a picture of Father Frost and glue glitter on top to make it shiny and festive.

Photo by Jeanne Stahl.

St. Basil's Cathedral

Photo by Jeanne Stahl.

RECIPES

*Borscht**

(approximate measurements—vary them if you wish)

8 beef boullion cubes
6 C. water
2 T. butter
½ chopped onion
1 large bay leaf
1 clove
1½ C. tomato juice
½ C. (can) sauerkraut and juice
1 C. cut beets
1 C. cut potatoes
1 C. cut carrots, parsley and/or celery tops
6 peppercorns

Combine water, bay leaf, clove, peppercorns, bouillon cubes, onion and butter to make a broth. Simmer about 2 hours.

Add parsley, celery tops, carrots, then tomato juice and sauerkraut. Then add beets, potatoes and more water, if necessary.

If you desire, you may add shredded cabbage and tomatoes. Continue cooking until done to taste. Serve with a large spoonful of sour cream in each bowl. If you want, serve dark bread and butter or cream cheese with the borscht for a complete Russian meal.

Cabbage

Russians eat lots of cabbage. You may fix it in a variety of ways. Steamed cabbage with a dash of vinegar and salt is an easy method of preparing cabbage.

VOCABULARY

Aeroflot—Russian airline
balalaika—guitar-like musical instrument
Bolsheviks—Communist group led by Lenin
Bolshoi—Russia's famous ballet company
borscho—vegetable soup made from beetroot and cabbage
caviar—the eggs of the sturgeon fish, a famous delicacy
cosmonaut—Russian astronaut
KGB—The State Committee on Security (secret police)
Kvass—Traditional Russian drink, rye beer
Lenin metro—Moscow's underground railroad
Matryoshka—series of wooden dolls which fit inside each other
Pioneers—Organization for young people
Pravda—newspaper published by Central Committee of the Communist party
Samovar—Russian tea urn
Soyuz—two-man spacecraft of the 1970's that joined the U.S. Apollo in space
Sputnik—artificial satellite
Tass—the official Russian news agency
troika—three-horse sled
Tsar (zar)—title of emperor in Old Russian
ushanka—Russian fur hat with ear flaps
vodka—Russian's national drink, distilled from rye

Russian Alphabet

А а	= a as in ark	П п	= p
Б б	= b	Р р	= r
В в	= v	С с	= s
Г г	= g as in gold	Т т	= t
Д д	= d	У у	= oo as in moon
Е е	= ye as in yellow	Ф ф	= f
ё	= yo as in yonder	Х х	= ch as in loch
Ж ж	= zh	Ц ц	= ts
З з	= z	Ч ч	= ch as in church
И и	= ee as in weed	Ш ш	= sh
й	= i (tenser than i in wit)	Щ щ	= sh followed by consonantal y
К к	= k		
Л л	= l	ы	= i as in wit
М м	= m	Э э	= e as in pet
Н н	= n	Ю ю	= u as in unicorn
О о	= o as in torn	Я я	= ya as in yarn

BIBLIOGRAPHY

NOTE: Where a recipe included in the text of any particular section was adapted from a written source, that source has been marked with an asterisk (*).

Introduction
Tarrow, Norma Bernstein and Lundsteen, Sara Wynn. *Activities and Resources for Guiding Young Children's Learning.* New York: McGraw Hill, 1981.

New England
Caballero, Jane. *Vanilla Manila Folder Games for Young Children.* Atlanta: Humanics Limited, 1980.

Indian Tribes
Bahti, Tom. *Southwestern Indian Arts and Crafts.* Las Vegas: K.C. Publications, 1966.

Alaska
Haywood, Charles. *Folk Songs of the World.* New York: John Day Co., Inc., 1966.

Canada
Barclay, Isabel. *O, Canada!* New York: Doubleday & Co., Inc., 1964.

Hunt, Sarah Ethridge. *Games and Sports Around the World.* New York: The Ronald Press Co., 1964.

Lineweaver, Charles and Lineweaver, Marion. *The First Book of Canada.* New York: Franklin Watts, Inc., 1955.

Moore, Brian. *Life World Library Canada.* New York: Time, Inc., 1963.

Ward, Lynd and McNeer, May. *The Canadian Story.* New York: Ariel Books, 1958.

*"Cuisine." *Montreal.* May, 1980.

China
*Cooper, Terry Touff and Ratner, Marilyn. *Many Hands Cooking.* New York: Thomas Y. Crowell Co., 1974.

Cressy, George. *Land of 500 Million: A Geography of China.* New York: McGraw Hill Book Co.,1955.

Halsey, W.D. "China." *Collier's Encyclopedia,* vol. 16. 1976.

Japan
Vaughn, *The Land and People of Japan.* New York: J.B. Lippincott and Co.

The New Book of Knowledge. New York: Grolier, Inc.

The World Book Encyclopedia. Chicago: Field Enterprises Educational Corporation.

Thailand
Country Project Kit of Thailand (no. 1026). New York: UNICEF.

The Royal Thai Embassy, Office of Public Relations Attache. 2300 Kalorama Rd., N.W., Washington, D.C. 20003.

World Wings International Hostess Cookbook. Independence, Mo.: Commemorative Cook Books, 1973.

Hawaii
Caballero, Jane. *Month by Month Activity Guide for the Primary Grades.* Atlanta: Humanics Limited, 1981.

Vietnam
Vu Quy Ky, Vietnamese national.

Atlas of the World. National Geography Society: Washington, D.C., 1966.

Embassy of Vietnam. *An Introduction to Vietnam.* Washington, D.C.

National Geographic. National Geography Society: Washington, D.C., 1978.

Webster's Seventh New Collegiate Dictionary. Springfield, Mass.: G. and C. Merriam Co., 1971.

The World Book Encyclopedia, vol. 20. The Scott and Fetzer Co. 1981.

Bahamas
Unsworth, Sister Virginia. *A History of the Bahamas.* St. Augustine's College, 1971.

Haiti
*Cooper, Terry Touff and Ratner, Marilyn. *Many Hands Cooking.* New York: Thomas Y. Crowell Co., 1974.

Dobrin, Arnold. *Josephine's Imagination. A Tale of Haiti.* New York: Scholastic Book Services, 1973.

**World Wings International Hostess Cook Book.* Independence, Mo.: Commemorative Cook Books, 1973.

Jamaica
Futch, John. "Jamaica on the Rebound—Soon Come." *The Atlanta Journal, The Atlanta Constitution.* Sunday, March 2, 1980.

World Wings International Hostess Cook Book. Independence, Mo.: Commemorative Cook Books, 1973.

Panama
Carlton, Michael. "Sailing Through Panama Canal is Exhilarating." *The Atlanta Journal, The Atlanta Constitution.* Sunday, February 1, 1981.

World Wings International Hostess Cook Book. Independence, Mo.: Commemorative Cook Books, 1973..

Mexico
Harris, Jane. *Dance A While.* Minneapolis: Burgess Publishing Co., 1955.

Brazil
*Cooper, Terry Touff and Ratner, Marilyn. *Many Hands Cooking.* New York: Thomas Y. Crowell Co., 1974.

Ceuta/Morroco
World Wings International Hostess Cook Book. Independence, Mo.: Commemorative Cook Books, 1973.

**Cooper, Terry Touff and Ratner, Marilyn. *Many Hands Cooking.* New York: Thomas Y. Crowell Co., 1974.

Kenya
**Country Project Kit on Kenya. New York: UNICEF. (331 East 38th St.)

World Wings International Hostess Cook Book. Independence, Mo.: Commemorative Cook Books, 1973.

Nigeria
Obediah A. Oriaku, Nigerian national.

*Cooper, Terry Touff and Ratner, Marilyn. *Many Hands Cooking.* New York: Thomas Y. Crowell Co., 1974.

India
World Wings International Hostess Cook Book. Independence, Mo.: Commemorative Cook Books, 1973.

Iran
*Borghase, Anita. *The International Cookie Jar Cookbook.* New York: Charles Scribner's Sons, 1975.

**Mazda, Maiden. *In a Persian Kitchen.* Japan: Charles E. Tuttle Co., 1960.

"Iran" *Collier's Encyclopedia,* vol. 13. 1970.

Iran. The General Department of Publications and Broadcasting.

"Iran." *Land and People,* vol. 13. Baltic States and Central Europe: Grollier, Inc., 1964.

"Iran." Reader's Digest 1981 Almanac & Yearbook. Reader's Digest Ass'n Inc., 1981.

Israel
Harris, Jane A., Pittman, Anne and Waller, Marlys. *Dance A While.* Minneapolis: Burgess Publishing Co., 1968.

Spain
Loder, Dorothy. *The Land and People of Spain.* New York: Lippincott, 1972.

Manning, Jack. *Young Spain.* New York: Dodd, Mead and Co., 1961.

Italy
Caballero, Jane. *The Handbook of Learning Activities.* Atlanta: Humanics Limited, 1981.

Epstein, Beryl and Epstein, Sam. *The First Book of Italy.* New York: Franklin Watts, Inc., 1972.

Geis, Darlene. *Let's Travel in Italy.* Chicago: Children's Press, Inc., 1964.

Gidal, Sonia and Gidal, Tim. *My Village in Italy.* New York: Random House, 1962.

Kish, George, *Life in Europe: Italy.* Grand Rapids: The Fideler Co., 1958.

Switzerland

Caballero, Jane. *Art Projects for Young Children.* Atlanta: Humanics Limited, 1980.

Kubly, Merbert. *Switzerland.* New York: Time Life, Inc., 1969.

The World Book Encyclopedia. Chicago: Field Enterprises Educational Corporation, 1964.

France

Trust Company of Georgia. International Division: France.

Netherlands

Caballero, Jane. *Month by Month Activity Guide for the Primary Grades.* Atlanta: Humanics Limited, 1981.

Consultant General of the Netherlands

Germany

Harbin, E.O. *Games of Many Nations.* Nashville: Abingdon Press.

Collier's Encyclopedia. New York: MacMillan Educational Corp., 1980.

The Encyclopedia Americana. Danbury, Connecticut, 1980.

The World Book Encyclopedia. New York: World Book Childcraft International, Inc., 1980.

Scotland, England, Wales

*Cooper, Terry Touff and Ratner, Marilyn. *Many Hands Cooking.* New York: Thomas Y. Crowell Co., 1974.

Ethridegehunt, Sarah. *Games and Sports the World Around.* New York: The Ronald Press, Co.

Rombeuer, Irma and Becker, Marion. *Joy of Cooking.* New York: The Bobbs-Merrill Co., Inc., 1979.

**World Wings International Hostess Cook Book.* Independence, Mo.: Commemorative Cook Books, 1973.

The World Book Encyclopedia. New York: World Book Childcraft International, Inc., 1980.

Ireland

Caballero, Jane. *Month by Month Activity Guide for the Primary Grades.* Atlanta: Humanics Limited, 1981.

World Wings International Hostess Cook Book. Independence, Mo.: Commemorative Cook Books, 1973.

Denmark, Finland, Sweden, Norway

Becker, Marion and Rambauer, Irma. *Joy of Cooking.* New York: The Bobbs-Merrill Co., Inc., 1979.

Wither, Jim. *Getting to Know Scandinavia.* New York: Coward-McCann, Inc., 1963.

World Wings International Hostess Cook Book. Independence, Mo.: Commemorative Cook Books, 1973.

"Sweden." *Land and People.* vol. 2. Baltic States and Cental Europe: Grolier, Inc., 1964.

Stockholm. National Geographic, vol, 149, no. 1, January, 1976.

"Sweden." *Reader's Digest 1981 Almanac & Yearbook.* Reader's Digest Ass'n Inc., 1981.

"Sweden." *World Book Encyclopedia,* vol. 16. New York: World Book Childcraft International. Inc., 1963.

Greece

Harbin, E.O. *Games of Many Nations.* Nashville: Abingdon Press.

Three Rivers Cookbook. Sewickley, Pennsylvania: Child Health Association of Sewickley, Inc.

Collier's Encyclopedia. New York: MacMillan Educational Corp., 1980.

The Encyclopedia Americana. Danbury, Connectticut: 1980.

The World Book Encyclopedia. New York: World Book Childcraft International, Inc., 1980.

Russia

World Wings International Hostess Cook Book. Independence, Mo.: Commemorative Cook Books, 1973.

SUGGESTED RECORDS

Aloha Oe. Masaaki Hirao and the Waikiki Hawaiians. Honolulu: Waikiki Records.

A Child's Introduction to Spanish. Carlos Montalban. Hudson Productions, Inc. Distributed by: New York: Affiliated Publishers, 1961.

Classical Indian Music. Yahudi Menuhin. New York: London Records Inc.

The Guru (sitar) Ustad Khan. New York: R.C.A., 1969.

It's a Small World, Walt Disney Productions, U.S.A.: Western Publishing Co., 1968.

Missa Luba. Congonese Boys' Choir. Baudouin.

The Religious Sounds of Tibet. (Buddhist hymns recorded in Tibetan monasteries in Northern India). West Germany: Teldec Telefunken Decca Schallplatten, Ges. mbH.

Russian Folk Songs. V. Andreyev Russian Folk Orchestra. U.S.S.R.

Travellin' With Ella Jenkins. New York: Folkways Records and Service Corp., 1979.

Yellow Bird. Jamaica Duke and the Mento Swingers. Jamaica, West Indies: Dynamic Sounds Recording Co. Ltd.

Children's Literature Around the World

A Story, A Story, an African tale retold and illustrated by Haley, Gail E. Hartford: Connecticut Printers, Inc., 1970. The 'spider story' tells how small, defenseless men or animals outwit others and succeed against great odds.

Big Blue Marble Atlas, Brown, Paula S. and Garrison, Robert L. NY: Ideals Publishing Corp., 1980. An atlas of the earth including information about outer space.*

Children's Art, Goldin, Rafael and Alla, The Foundation of Children's History, Art and Culture, SOS Children's Villages, 1981. Children's art from around the world.

Children Around the World, Troop, Miriam, NY: Grosset and Dunlap, Inc., 1964. Sketches include children in various countries illustrated in water color.

Children of the North Pole (Greenland), Herrmanns, Ralph, NY: Harcourt, Brace and World, 1963. Unexpected help comes to little Serkok who has lost his father's kayak while hunting for seals.

Children of Viet-nam, Tran-Khanh-Tuyet, Washington, DC; Indochina Resource Center. A picture storybook with pen and ink.

Chants for Children, Colgin, Mary Lou, NY: Colgin Publishing Co., 1982. A collection of rhymes and ditties; animals, abc's, nursery rhymes, holidays and seasons.*

The Five Chinese Brothers, Bishop, Clair Huchet and Wise, Kurt. Coward-McCann, Inc., 1938. A folktale, rich in wit and humor.

Ganga, retold by Seshadri, Lakshmi. Bombay: India Book House Education Trust. The legend of the most sacred river of India.

Havoc in Heaven, Cheng, Tang. Beijing: Foreign Languages Press, 1979. Based on a color cartoon film drawn from a sixteenth century fantasy novel.

How India Won Her Freedom, Chaitanya, Krishna. India: National Book Trust, 1973. The story of how the people of India lost their freedom to Britain and how they fought for many years to win their freedom back.

It's a Small World, Walt Disney Productions; USA: Western Publishing Co., Inc., 1968. The story of an orphan boy's journey through Disneyland.

Jewaharlal Nehru, Gatha, Gaurav. New Delhi: Jay Print Pack, 1981. Nehru was the first prime minister of India and maintained the office for 17 years.

Johnny-Cake, Jacobs, Joseph, NY: G.P. Putnam's Sons, 1933. An English fairy tale.

Josephine's Imagination, Dobrin, Arnold. NY: Scholastic Book Services, 1975. A young Haitian girl uses her imagination while walking to the market with her mother.

Let's Travel in India, Geis, Darlene. NY: Children's Press, Inc., 1965. This teacher resource book contains maps, pictures and information about India.*

Little Toot on the Mississippi, Gramotky, Hardie. NY: G.P. Putnam's Sons, 1973. When the Mississippi River goes into flood, adventure-loving Little Toot sets out on a daring rescue mission.

Madeline's Rescue, Bemelman's Ludwig. NY: The Viking Press, 1953. Rhymed text about the story of Madeline's rescue and her rescuer, Genevive. (French)

Mahabharata, Pai, Anant. Bombay: H.G. Mirchandani for India Book House Education Trust. This book in comic book form tells of the longest epic poem in the world.

Nine Days to Christmas, Ets, Marie Hall and Labastida, Aurora. NY: The Viking Press, 1959. Ceci, a little Mexican girl is excited because she is old enough to buy a pinata for her first Christmas pasada.

Peter and the Wolf, Writ, Arthur. NY: Telebooks, 1983. Peter, disobeying his grandfather, went into the woods to hunt for a wolf.

Saint George and the Dragon, Hodges, Margaret. Boston: Little, Brown and Co., 1984. A segment from Spencer's "The Fairie Queen" is retold.

Sing, Children, Sing, Bernstein, Leonard, NY: Chappell and Co., Inc., 1972. In an arrangement with UNICEF, a collection of songs, dances and singing games from many countries.

The Story of Ping, Flack, Marjorie and Wises, Kurt, NY: The Viking Press, 1933. Ping runs away from his houseboat on the Yangtze River. (Chinese)

The Story of Ramayan, retold by Choudhry, Bani Roy. New Delhi; Hemkunt Press, 1981. The epic tale of India.

Wash 'em Clean, Chuckousky, Karnei. Moscow: Progress Publishers. A story in poetic form telling of a little boy who wakes up to find all of his items around him running away because he is so dirty.

(*Teacher Resource)

The Successful Teacher's Most Valuable Resource!

EDUCATION

THE EARLI PROGRAM
Excellent language development program! Volume I contains developmentally sequenced lessons in verbal receptive language; Volume II, expressive language. Use as a primary, supplemental or rehabilitative language program.

Volume I	HL-067-7	$14.95
Volume II	HL-074-X	$14.95

LEARNING ENVIRONMENTS FOR CHILDREN
A practical manual for creating efficient, pleasant and stressfree learning environments for children centers. Make the best possible use of your center's space!

HL-065-0 $12.95

COMPETENCIES:
A Self-Study Guide to Teaching Competencies in Early Childhood Education
This comprehensive guide is ideal for evaluating or improving your competency in early childhood education or preparing for the CDA credential.

HL-024-3 $14.95

ENERGY:
A Curriculum for 3, 4 and 5 Year Olds
Help preschool children become aware of what energy is, the sources of energy, the uses of energy and wise energy use with the fun-filled activities, songs and games included in this innovative manual.

HL-069-3 $ 9.95

YOUNG CHILDREN'S BEHAVIOR:
Implementing Your Goals
A variety of up-to-date approaches to discipline and guidance to help you deal more effectively with children. Also an excellent addition to CDA and competency-based training programs.

HL-015-4 $ 8.95

FINGERPLAYS & RHYMES
Delight children 2-8 while teaching them about numbers, colors, shapes, holidays, self-concept, feelings, and much more. More than 250 original rhymes and fingerplays.

HL-083-9 $14.95

STORYBOOK CLASSROOMS:
Using Children's Literature in the Learning Center/Primary Grades
A guide to making effective use of children's literature in the classroom. Activities designed for independent use by children K – 3, supplemented with illustrations and patterns for easy use. Guidelines, suggestions, and bibliographies will delight and help to instill a love of reading in kids!

HL-043-X $16.95

ACTIVITY BOOKS

EARLY CHILDHOOD ACTIVITIES:
A Treasury of Ideas from Worldwide Sources
A virtual encyclopedia of projects, games and activities for children aged 3 – 7, containing over 500 different child-tested activities drawn from a variety of teaching systems. The ultimate activity book!

HL-066-9 $16.95

VANILLA MANILA FOLDER GAMES
Make exciting and stimulating **Vanilla Manila Folder Games** quickly and easily with simple manila file folders and colored marking pens. Unique learning activities designed for children aged 3 – 8.

HL-059-6 $16.95

LEAVES ARE FALLING IN RAINBOWS
Science Activities for Early Childhood
Hundreds of science activities help your children learn concepts an properties of water, air, plants, light, shadows, magnets, sound and elec tricity. Build on interests when providing science experience and they'll **always** be eager to learn!

HL-045-6 $16.95

HANDBOOK OF LEARNING ACTIVITIES
Over 125 exciting, enjoyable activities and projects for young children in the areas of math, health and safety, play, movement, science, social studies, art, language development, puppetry and more!

HL-058-8 $16.95

MONTH BY MONTH ACTIVITY GUIDE FOR THE PRIMARY GRADES
Month by Month gives you a succinct guide to the effective recruitment and utilization of teachers' aides plus a **full year's worth** of fun-filled education activities in such areas as reading, math, art, and science.

HL-061-8 $16.95

ART PROJECTS FOR YOUNG CHILDREN
Build a basic art program of stimulating projects on a limited budget and time schedule with **Art Projects**. Contains over 100 fun-filled projects in the areas of drawing, painting, puppets, clay, printing and more!

HL-051-0 $16.95

BLOOMIN' BULLETIN BOARDS
Stimulate active student participation and learning as you promote your kids' creativity with these delightful and entertaining activities in the areas of Art, Language Arts, Mathematics, Health, Science, Social Studies, and the Holidays. Watch learning skills and self-concepts blossom!

HL-047-2 $14.95

AEROSPACE PROJECTS FOR YOUNG CHILDREN
Introduce children to the fascinating field of aerospace with the exciting and informative projects and field trip suggestions. Contributors include over 30 aviation/aerospace agencies and personnel.

HL-052-9 $14.95

CHILD'S PLAY:
An Activities and Materials Handbook
An eclectic selection of fun-filled activities for preschool children designed to lend excitement to the learning process. Activities include puppets, mobiles, poetry, songs and more.

HL-003-0 $14.95

READING RESOURCE BOOK
This excellent, highly readable text gives you an overview of children's language development, suggestions for games that enhance reading skills, ideas for establishing a reading environment in the home, tips for grandparents, and lists of resources.

HL-044-8 $16.95

HUMANICS LEARNING

Storybook Classrooms
Using Children's Literature In the Learning Center
Karla Hawkins Wendelin, Ph.D. • M. Jean Greenlaw, Ph.D.

the leaves are falling in rainbows
Michael E. Knight, Ph.D.
Terry L. Graham, M.A.
Science Activities for Early Childhood

bloomin' bulletin boards
Elaine Commins, M.Ed.

Reading Resource Book
Parents & Beginning Reading

Humanics Publications

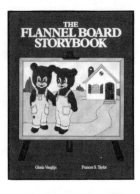

CHILDREN AROUND THE WORLD
Introduce preschool and kindergarten children to people and ways of other cultures.
HL-033-2 $16.95

THE FLANNELBOARD STORYBOOK
Step-by-step directions, story-telling techniques and how to make flannelboards and materials.
HL-093-6 $16.95

BIRTHDAYS: A CELEBRATION
More than 30 party themes and 200 games and activites are adaptable for children ages 3–10.
HL-075-8 $14.95

TEDDY BEARS AT SCHOOL
Learning center activities centered around teddy bears includes math, fine and gross motor skills, self concept and more. Ages 4–7
HL-092-8 $16.95

THE LOLLIPOP TEST
A Diagnostic Screening Test of School Readiness
Based on the latest research in school readiness, this test effectively measures children's readiness strengths and weaknesses. Included is all you need to give, score and interpret the test.
HL-028-6   (Specimen Set) $29.95

CAN PIAGET COOK?
Forty-six lesson plans with reproducible worksheets. Children experience science first hand with these food-related activities.
HL-078-2 $12.95

SCISSOR SORCERY
Over 50 reproducible, developmentally sequenced activity sheets help children learn to cut proficiently.
HL-076-6 $16.95

THE INFANT & TODDLER HANDBOOK
Activities for children birth to 24 months. For teachers, day care personnel, parents & other care givers.
HL-038-3 $12.95

TODDLERS LEARN BY DOING
Hundreds of activities are developmentally designed just for toddlers.
HL-085-5 $12.95

NUTS AND BOLTS
Guidelines for setting up an early learning center, organization and management.
HL-063-4 $ 8.95

THE CHILD CARE INVENTORY & MANUAL
Developed for infant & preschool programs. The Inventory reviews 11 performance areas. The manual explains how to collect, score and interpret the data.
HL-090-1   (Set) $19.95

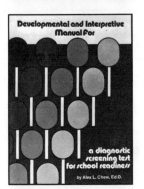

HUMANICS LEARNING

ORDER FORM

Send Orders To:

Humanics Learning
P.O. Box 7447
Atlanta, Ga. 30309

Name _____

Address _____

City _____ State _____ Zip _____

TITLE	CODE	PRICE	QUANTITY	TOTAL

All orders from individuals must include prepayment, or credit card number and signature must be provided below.

☐ MasterCard   ☐ Visa

_____
Account Number

_____
Signature

_____
MasterCard Interbank No.   Expiration Date

_____
Institutional Purchase Order

SUBTOTAL	
Ga. Residents, add 5% sales tax	
Discount, if applicable	
Shipping and Handling	
TOTAL	

☎ **ORDER TOLL FREE**
1-800-874-8844

- **Same Day Telephone Service —**
  Order toll free and we will ship your order within 48 hours.

- **Order By Phone —**
  with Visa or MasterCard

Shipping and Handling Charges

Up to $10.00 add	$2.00
$10.01 to $20.00 add	$3.00
$20.01 to $40.00 add	$4.00
$40.01 to $70.00 add	$5.00
$70.01 to $100.00 add	$6.00
$100.01 to $125.00 add	$7.00
$125.01 to $150.00 add	$8.00
$150.01 to $175.00 add	$9.00
$175.01 to $200.00 add	$10.00

Orders over $200 vary depending on method of shipment.

Please call for discounts and terms.